Praise fo

"*The Great Expectations Story* provides the background, vision, and hope for all schools truly dedicated to creating lifelong learners. It is a spectacular testament to the power of the collective intelligence of educators, relentlessly applied in the service of teaching and learning. Told from a wonderfully relaxed story-telling point of view, it is truly a joy to read."
—Rich Allen, PhD, Founder of Green Light Education
Author, educator, and master trainer

"Christy Sheffield has described Charlie Hollar's passion and vision of GE Model Schools in an excellent way. Charlie's vision was for all students to achieve success regardless of race, social economic status, or cultural conditioning. As the story tells in this book, GE Model Schools' teaching methodology insures that all students can learn and achieve success."
—Kent Lashley, PhD, Professor Emeritus
Northeastern State University, Oklahoma

The Great Expectations Story
*A TRANSFORMATION PLAN
FOR AMERICA'S SCHOOLS*

CHRISTY SHEFFIELD

The Great Expectations Story
Copyright © 2016
Great Expectations® Foundation, Inc.

ALL RIGHTS RESERVED
No portion of this publication may be reproduced, stored in any electronic system, or transmitted in any form or by any means, electronic, mechanical, photocopy, recording, or otherwise, without written permission from the author. Brief quotations may be used in literary reviews.

Cover art by Robert Daniel Victor Copu

ISBN : 978-0-9727138-5-6

GREAT EXPECTATIONS ® FOUNDATION, INC.
Northeastern State University
Tahlequah, OK 74464
918-444-3744
www.greatexpectations.org

Printed in the USA by
Morris Publishing®
3212 E. Hwy. 30
Kearney, NE 68847
800-650-7888
www.morrispublishing.com

Acknowledgements

Samuel Adams coined the expression to "give credit to whom credit is due" in a letter he wrote in 1777. It is still a valid concept, and the first line of acknowledgement prompted by this book is to all those woven into the history of Great Expectations who helped it become the vibrant organization that fulfills its promise to "transform lives through education."

Charlie Hollar's passionate dream of making education better for all learners was noted by colleagues, business associates, and lawmakers who caught the importance of Charlie's vision and then contributed their influence and, in some cases, their dollars. Selfless members of the Great Expectations Foundation Board have given hours of their lives and their dedicated contemplation of many matters in order to facilitate the operation of all aspects of the organization. Generous corporations have donated financially to make it possible for teachers to attend GE Summer Institute. Legislators have supported the work of Great Expectations by providing funding for teacher training. Community business leaders have embraced the high expectations that Great Expectations promotes and supported the same elevated standards in their businesses. The Great Expectations Leadership Team has labored with unflagging diligence to convey to educators "how to implement" all the beneficial intricacies of the GE Tenets, Expectations, and Practices. All of these individuals and entities are due credit for helping Great Expectations to continue to thrive and enrich lives.

There is one more important cadre of essential contributors to the success of Great Expectations. That group consists of the "ground level" GE educators. They are owed recognition and thanks because it is their day-to-day lives in the classrooms and administrative offices that have made Great Expectations a vigorous, constant influence that will make a lifelong difference in the lives of students.

Additionally, appreciation goes to all who contributed to the formulation of this book. As the one who set about to write the story of Great Expectations, I used my own experiences as a GE teacher, the observations I made during my years as a GE Instructional Coach, and mostly the responses to the many interviews I conducted.

Thanks goes to a former state school superintendent and her associates as well as to university presidents and professors who knew Charlie as he put forth ceaseless efforts to launch his ideas into reality. They gave firsthand accounts of his initial endeavors to make sure that the best practices in teaching would be adopted in classrooms.

Thanks to the Great Expectations Coaches and leaders for their descriptions of classroom observations and, also, for some of their first person reports of how GE was conceived and then developed and refined.

Further excellent insights came from GE instructors, teachers, principals, and superintendents who graciously shared narratives of the way GE operates in their schools.

And finally, some of the story about Great Expectations came from students who told how GE works from their vantage point.

Thank you to all who kindly shared their GE experiences for the telling of *The Great Expectations Story*. Thanks to all who've had a role in living Charlie's dream.

— Christy Sheffield

The Great Expectations Story

Acknowledgements .... *iii*

Section I: Great Expectations in Fact

How Great Expectations Got Its Start

    The Man Who Wouldn't Hear "No" 3

What Is Great Expectations Anyway?

    The Transformation Plan 11

    Beliefs: Basic Tenets 13

    Student Code of Conduct: Expectations for Living 15

    Blueprint for Teaching: Classroom Practices 16

    Core of Character Development: Life Principles 19

Substantiating Research on GE Effectiveness........................25

Voices from Great Expectations Schools: Case Studies 29

Section II: Great Expectations in Action

Prologue

    Vicarious Visit..59

Chapter 1

    New Year, New School, New Town 61

Chapter 2

    Expectations, Creeds, and Life Principles 67

Chapter 3

    In the Spotlight, Not on the Spot 85

Chapter 4

    Giving, and Giving Thanks 95

Chapter 5
    Consulting with a Coach 109

Chapter 6
    The "Beastly" Month of February 121

Chapter 7
    Maximizing March 139

Chapter 8
    Spring Fever and Specials 159

Chapter 9
    Learning Up to the Last Minute 175

Epilogue
    Summary of Successes 189

The Great Expectations Tree 195

Want to Know More? 197

About the Author 199

Section I
Great Expectations in Fact

Charlie Hollar

How Great Expectations Got Its Start

The Man Who Wouldn't Hear "No"

"What we need are more people who specialize in the impossible."
THEODORE ROETHKE

Great Expectations and the transformation of lives through education began with one man: Charles Hollar. Charlie – the name he much preferred over Mr. Hollar – was a successful businessman from Ponca City, Oklahoma, who, when he retired at age 55, was still full of energies, connections, and capabilities to be put to use. Though he was not an educator, he had read and been deeply moved by *A Nation at Risk: The Imperative For Educational Reform,* the 1983 report of President Ronald Reagan's National Commission on Excellence in Education. The report asserted that American schools were failing. Charlie was haunted by the serious conclusions in that report. He believed there was a crisis; he couldn't see schools getting better without some intervention. Under the weight of civic responsibility, he wanted to help teachers and administrators in their most difficult job. He seized the notion of helping education, not just in his local community, but in a manner that would truly benefit all children in Oklahoma and restore educators' sense of joy and accomplishment in teaching. As he thought about this fledging premise, he began to develop a dream of how education might be changed, and the more he read, researched, questioned, and discussed his concept of change, the more his commitment to the idea grew. He was touched by the possibilities of inspiring people to have a different view of what education could be.

In the early days of his vision, before any development of materials or methods, Charlie started with the highest education officer in Oklahoma, the Secretary of Education. Charlie would frequent the office at the state capitol, with (and more often, without) an appointment, asking for support and financial backing. He hoped for a state educational grant and sought help from the Governor. He sat in the outer office waiting room so consistently that the Governor finally asked his Secretary of Education, "Who is that white-haired man; does he work for us?"

Charlie's dream was never diminished by obstructions and denials of his requests. He just didn't hear "no." His own stated philosophy was "If you are involved in a passion, you do not see any of the obstacles; you just know where you are going."

The fire was truly kindled when Charlie was able to wangle signatures from both the Republican State Superintendent of Education and the Democratic State Superintendent Candidate on a letter to school principals. To whatever objections there might have been raised concerning hindrances to such bi-partisan support, Charlie's typical answer was, "Yes, I know, but this is important!" The letter explained Charlie's brainchild for educational reform and asked people to accompany him to Chicago to see firsthand an effective teaching model which had received nation-wide acclaim. And, yes, there were teachers, administrators, and other key figures in Oklahoma education who agreed to go on that trip.

The Chicago observation proved to be an adventure for Charlie and all those who had caught the excitement of his plan. The day of the trip departure, a fierce ice storm made driving to the airport slow and treacherous, but the traveling team members were so dedicated that they made their way to the airport anyway. Multiple de-icings, an unscheduled stop in St. Louis, and a near skid off the runway in Chicago merely heightened the anticipation for the auspicious undertaking.

As the group rode to the Chicago school where they were to observe the special teaching practices that had been honored in national media coverage, Charlie, who was bundled against the bitter cold, walked up and down the aisle of the charter bus with the earflaps on his fuzzy black Russian trooper hat flopping as he talked. His message was composed of excited words of encouragement. "We will change education in Oklahoma. What an opportunity awaits! The challenge is on our shoulders. We need to know what is best in education and bring about change."

After the observation in Chicago, Charlie's dream expanded and solidified. He gathered some educators to help compile the best practices in teaching and develop ways to explain those concepts to others. At a communication seminar which he set up, he was so excited that he couldn't sleep. He left notes on the participants' hotel doors at all hours of the night, asking questions or commenting on ideas from the previous day, and yet when the first person made his way to get coffee at 5:30 AM each morning, he would find Charlie there wanting to talk about how to share the goal of excellence.

Charlie did not just tell people what was to be done, he made leaders, teachers, and administrators think through what was needed to accomplish their goals. The colleagues who were a part of that early communication seminar were sequestered with grueling training. Charlie was adamant; they must learn to convey ideas and strategies clearly. If they were to change the status quo in Oklahoma education, they needed more than knowledge; they must be able to impart the necessary steps forward. He insisted that people think critically: evaluate and apply ideas, deduce consequences from what is known, and make use of information to solve problems.

For example, at the seminar, Charlie gave his hand-picked crew of educational leaders a puzzle challenge. Teams were given 1000-piece jigsaw puzzles and a time limit for getting the puzzles put together completely. Each team had to come up with its own strategy. Because of the demands of the task, participants were forced to move away from "the way we have always done" jigsaw puzzles and reach out to extra resources. One team even called the puzzle publisher to ask questions about the intricacies of puzzle design to assist in getting all the pieces in place by the time deadline. After the test, the groups were led to realize what a metaphor the jigsaw puzzle assembly was for the task of education and for changing the existing mediocrity – many pieces have to fit together smoothly, faculty members must cooperate, extraordinary resources may need to be called in, and all must be accomplished before the minutes of the school year quickly drain away.

There were many other challenges encountered in that seminar, and those experiences became a model for the work of the Great Expectations Leadership team: focus on the goal, assure a clear interchange of ideas, work together, look past what seems impossible, and find a way to achieve excellence. Great Expectations began to develop as a teacher professional development training entity emphasizing high expectations, building self-esteem, believing that all children can learn, creating a climate of mutual respect, and underscoring the importance of teacher attitude and teacher knowledge and skill.

From those early plans evolved many aspects of Great Expectations: training at Summer Institute, conferences, implementation of Great Expectations practices in schools, guidance from experienced GE coaches, training for administrators, and learners who achieve academic excellence as they thrive in a school culture of respect.

Though Charlie died in the fall of 2011 of a rare and aggressive form of leukemia, his tenacity and fierce enthusiasm for improving education for all children are still a driving force of Great Expectations.

He was a tall man with a lean build that matched his college history as a runner, and his pure white hair added to his striking appearance. His presence was ubiquitous at Summer Institute sessions where he visited classes in progress, interviewed teachers on what they had been learning, and urged instructors to go for walks in the evening when he would tout his reading list and promote enriched vocabulary. "What have you been reading lately?" he would ask, or "How do you build vocabulary?" He purchased loads of important books, handed them out, and said, "Here, read this!"

He seemed tireless, though he was once discovered taking a nap on the comfy carpet underneath the registration table on an afternoon when training participants were all busy in class. Another time, he showed up at a Summer Institute opening session wearing layers and layers of t-shirts. He had put on the shirts for each of the twenty summers that there had been GE sessions. He crisscrossed the state to visit teachers in their classrooms and to relish the impressive accomplishments of students. He logged many miles of driving, all in his own car and at his own expense, including the unnecessary miles that he drove when he got lost on his way to some school site.

He continued his efforts to enlist the assistance of legislators, businessmen, influential community members, and affluent acquaintances; he collected friends of accomplishment, talent, and political leadership. He brought an endless string of guests – including news media, governors' wives, and a representative of the U.S. Department of Education – to be impressed by the stellar training in the summer sessions. He sought out people of excellence to serve as Great Expectations leaders, coaches, and instructors. He recruited a professor who was an Endowed Chair for Teaching Excellence at Northeastern State University to be a spokesperson for GE. He wanted to enlist "the best of the best."

Charlie looked for ways to support the needs of administrators by establishing Principals' Academy, which was designed to provide leadership training. For that endeavor, he tapped the talents of an international coaching consultant who provides similar training for management professionals in corporations. He founded the Educators' Leadership Academy for teachers and administrators in K-12 schools as well as in career-tech and higher education. He sought connections with college professors and researchers. He rounded up corporate sponsors whose contributions continue to have a huge impact on financing training. He invited prestigious book authors to come for presentations to GE participants, and he sent Great Expectations leaders and coaches to premier training sessions across the country to make sure the information GE was sharing with teachers matched with the latest information on the best practices in education.

Charlie assembled a tremendously talented Great Expectations Foundation Board of Directors, with additional support from Advisory Board Members. He searched out ways to obtain studies and research to validate GE's effectiveness. He had conversations with all the Oklahoma governors as different leaders rotated through that head position in the state, because his purposes did not have to do with party politics.

Charlie was certainly not focused on creating a program for its profit potential, and he himself received no compensation for all his time and effort. However, money was on his mind because he worked tirelessly to round up funding so that teachers and administrators could afford to attend GE training. He was often told "discouraging words," but his conviction was irrepressible. His thought was "There must be a way because we've got to get money for schools." He wasn't stopped by someone's saying, "No, that funding is not possible." He either willed away or worked away such barriers.

In hopes of accessing federal funding, he made trips to Washington, D.C., and met with the U.S. Department of Education. He made one such trip shortly after the terrorist bombing of the World Trade Center had cast a frightening pall over air travel. Charlie's flight arrived in D.C. long past midnight, and his luggage had been lost. Charlie was unperturbed. He met with the U.S. Secretary of Education having had little sleep, wearing his travel clothes, and grooming himself without his razor. However, it was all great as far as Charlie was concerned because he eventually gained approval for schools to apply not only Title II, but also Title I Federal Funds to GE Training.

On one occasion, Charlie was a visitor in a GE Summer Institute class. The activity of the day fit with the Great Expectations Basic Tenet of Building Self-Esteem. Participants were asked to sketch a picture of their favorite living thing other than a person, and then to turn the paper over and write five adjectives that described that favorite living thing. Usually the chosen descriptive words actually fit the person as well as the favorite thing because the characteristics were ones the person admired. Charlie drew a picture of Dudley Do Right, his golden cocker spaniel; Dudley gave him joy each time he made it back home. The adjectives Charlie gave to describe Dudley were *Loving, Energetic, Playful, Friendly,* and *Smart.* Those were all very suitable terms to apply to Charlie also!

Additionally, Charlie must be described as a lifelong learner, and one with the capability to make others feel important, unique, and special. He cared about helping the less fortunate. He once spoke of his mother and the impressive things she had accomplished; she surely would have been proud of his intense dedication to take education to new heights and to make excellence possible for all children. He inspired others and, over two decades, arguably had more influence than anyone else on Oklahoma education.

Charlie's years of perseverance in establishing Great Expectations have paid off. As of this writing, there are Model GE Schools in Oklahoma, Texas, Kansas, and Michigan. There are many additional school sites where diligent teachers are in the development phase of implementing the GE Practices. Over 52,000 educators have been trained in GE Methodology, and roughly 250,000 students are being taught by a GE-trained teacher. There are lives being transformed through education.

As Charlie watched GE serve more and more people, he began to speak of having a book to tell about Great Expectations. We are not in the habit of telling Charlie, "No," since he would not even hear that word anyway, so here is the book. Study through the explanation of the components of the program, examine the research that validates the success of the practitioners, and review the accounts from administrators where Great Expectations is a part of day-to-day life. Then turn to Section II to gain the perspective of a family that moves to a community where Great Expectations is a way of life.

Thanks to Charlie for giving us Great Expectations!

What Is Great Expectations Anyway?

The Transformation Plan

Great Expectations is a stellar teacher professional development program that utilizes research-based advice on the best practices in teaching to aid teachers in honing their teaching methodology. Great Expectations teachers and administrators guide all students to strive for excellence in academic accomplishment and in admirable character development.

Great Expectations (GE) is firmly based on research of the best practices in teaching, and it is kept continually in tune with those best practices by means of the ongoing advice and the most recent reports of research found in current educational publications. Presentations and articles by educational authors and consultants are continually examined for the prevailing wisdom on how best to teach. This ongoing review of the latest research keeps Great Expectations fresh and helps to maximize the benefit of GE training.

The main objectives of Great Expectations when it is put into practice are to increase students' self-esteem, boost their academic knowledge and learning competence, and build their social proficiency and worth as citizens. To accomplish these high-level goals, GE focuses on the transformation of educators by means of intensive training and the metamorphosis of schools through a refinement in the day-to-day educational interactions. Educators are assisted in re-examining their teaching methods and dealings with students and guided in evaluating, and perhaps redefining, their values and beliefs about student learning.

Teachers are able to ratchet up their students' academic standing by following the GE practices of reviewing concepts; integrating subject areas; providing links between present, past, and future lessons; expanding critical thinking skills; and developing enriched vocabulary. Especially useful to GE teachers is the application of insights stemming from brain research on learning. As an added benefit, teacher strategies are thoughtfully chosen to facilitate students' personal motivation.

As Great Expectations is implemented, fully and richly, it changes not only the teaching and learning processes at schools, but it also colors the lives of teachers, students, and administrators. For example, teachers and students memorize and reference quotations that succinctly provide advice on one's personal attitudes and actions; these sage recommendations from the ages help define a mindset of determination, optimism, and resilience. Students are taught to fulfill classroom expectations so that they mature into young people who consistently treat others with respect. Even the words from student mouths demonstrate courtesy, and student creeds set up goals of excellence and integrity. These effects of high standards of performance and personal qualities of good character can even spill over into homes and businesses in the communities where Great Expectations is utilized. Some GE teachers say "Great Expectations is a way of life;" and this explains the appropriateness of the Great Expectations Slogan: "Transforming Lives Through Education."

Such transformations of lives begins for educators as they attend intensive, but encouraging, four-day professional development sessions. The shaping of teachers who are implementers of the GE program continues with other program elements which support application of the information from the training sessions. There are GE Coaches who work with schools and teachers to facilitate implementation, lead followup training sessions during the school year, and sustain opportunities to communicate and interact with like-minded educators. Additional classes and conferences sharpen interest and offer fresh recommendations to practitioners. The camaraderie with other GE colleagues yields encouragement and helps to cement commitment to utilizing the strategies presented in training.

Beliefs

The facets of Great Expectations can be delineated into two areas: Academic Excellence and a Culture of Respect. The goals of nurturing student learning and maturing young people into productive and upstanding citizens rests on the underpinnings of the Great Expectations beliefs of what must happen in education. Each of these beliefs springs from and is substantiated by many pieces of research.

Great Expectations begins with the judgment that **all students can learn**, no matter what labels have been placed on them or what personal challenges they face. There is no single magical step that will eliminate the gaps in achievement that rob some students of their future in society, but schools that effectively implement high-leverage strategies with fidelity can get results. GE prompts educators to find a way to help every student work up to his or her potential.

A second GE belief is in the need for teachers to hold **high expectations** of students and to communicate those expectations to the students themselves. Holding high expectations is the anticipation of excellence in performance, the focus on rising to new levels of personal best, and the determination that mediocrity is not satisfactory. The teachers need to strive for personal excellence themselves and then help students envision the highest possibilities for their studies, behavior, and interaction with others. GE urges teachers to coach students to face each new opportunity with the goal of doing their best.

Furthermore, Great Expectations adheres to the conviction that **building student self-esteem** is of crucial importance. Students with positive self-esteem see themselves as worthy and capable of high academic and social achievement. Their whole approach to studies is impacted because they have a can-do attitude, and overall they conduct themselves in a more admirable and cooperative manner because they perceive themselves as unique, competent, and connected to others.

Additionally, Great Expectations has considered the research on the qualities of highly productive business organizations and holds the conviction that the same factors of a **climate of mutual respect** apply to the school setting. GE pushes to the forefront the urgency of teachers' respecting students and of teachers' inclusion of a number of crucial measures to make sure students extend respect to all the others in the school setting – administrators, teachers, classmates, support staff, and themselves!

GE postulates, based on research as always, that educators themselves are a critical factor in the operation of education. Great Expectations emboldens teachers by helping them to embrace the importance of **teacher attitude, responsibility, knowledge, and skill.** Each teacher is the decisive element in the class setting where he or she is offering education.

These six Great Expectations Basic Tenets combine to produce the innovative outcome of an educational environment where students experience a school atmosphere of civility, kindness, courtesy, and dignity so that they can climb a scholastic ladder to educational distinction.

Six Basic Tenets

All Children Can Learn
High Expectations
Building Self-Esteem
Climate of Mutual Respect
Teacher Attitude and Responsibility
Teacher Knowledge and Skill

Student Code of Conduct

Great Expectations students are guided by a type of student code rather than being asked to follow school or classroom rules. The code of student conduct, which is called the **Eight Expectations for Living**, protects the smooth operation of all the activities at schools whether the students are in the classroom, cafeteria, sports arena, assembly space, hallway, or special event venue. The expectations support the desired respectful environment, promote good fellowship and citizenship, and advance healthy self-esteem. The expectations become so ingrained that students continue to practice them beyond the walls of the school. As they memorize the expectations and employ them consistently, the students become the police for the conduct guidelines and frequently call for their enforcement themselves. Educators can refer to the short list as hard and fast reminders for any student who fails to live up to the expectations. They are invaluable in helping students own their behavior rather than seeking to shift blame for problems or failings to someone else, and when a classroom of pupils are all adhering to the expectations, the desired Culture of Respect flourishes.

Eight Expectations for Living

1. We will value one another as unique and special individuals.
2. We will not laugh at or make fun of a person's mistakes nor use sarcasm or putdowns.
3. We will use good manners, saying "please," "thank you," and "excuse me" and allow others to go first.
4. We will cheer each other to success.
5. We will help one another whenever possible.
6. We will recognize every effort and applaud it.
7. We will encourage each other to do our best.
8. We will practice virtuous living, using the Life Principles.

Blueprint for Teaching Methodology

Great Expectations sets forth a plan – a blueprint – for teachers' methodology through 17 carefully crafted classroom practices. Each of the routines laid out by means of the practices are thoroughly substantiated by research as being the most effective manner of educating young people. The GE methodology is what's best for students. Learning is facilitated, and good conduct becomes ingrained because of the tactics that flow from the practices.

Each practice is an umbrella under which the application of effective education can take place. The execution of the practices varies somewhat depending upon the classroom grade level as well as upon the subject matter being taught, but the essence of the practices remains relevant whatever the setting.

GE training and coaching lead teachers to utilize a scaffolding plan for systematically putting all of the practices into use. Colleague advice and examples solidify each teacher's implementation. Administrators have a clear master plan for guiding all the educators in their school system.

Students are the ultimate winners at a Great Expectations school because rich, thorough implementation of the practices leads educators to be effective teachers, and students have the opportunity to do their best learning and to become young men and women of integrity.

17 Classroom Practices

1. Educators and learners model desired behaviors and attitudes such as those set forth in the Life Principles and the Eight Expectations for Living.

2. Educators and learners speak in complete sentences and address one another by name, demonstrating mutual respect and common courtesy.

3. Learners are taught thoroughly and to mastery, insuring success for all. Whole group instruction is interwoven with flexible group instruction and individual instruction.

4. Learning experiences are integrated, related to the real world, reviewed consistently, and connected to subsequent curricula.

5. Critical thinking skills are taught.

6. The environment is non-threatening and conducive to risk-taking. Mistakes are viewed as opportunities to learn and grow.

7. Memory work, recitations, and/or writing occur daily. These enhance character development and effective communication skills while extending curricula.

8. Enriched vocabulary is evident and is drawn directly from challenging writings, informational text, and/or wisdom literature.

9. The Magic Triad, a positive and caring environment, and discipline with dignity and logic are evident.

10. Learners' work is displayed in some form. Positive and timely feedback is provided through oral and/or written commentary.

11. Word identification skills are used as a foundation for expanding the use of the English language.

12. Learners assume responsibility for their own behavior. Their choices determine consequences.

13. A school, class, or personal creed is recited or reflected upon daily to reaffirm commitment to excellence.

14. All learners experience success. The educator guarantees it by comparing learners to their own past performance, not the performance of others. Learners are showcased, and past failures are disregarded.

15. Educators teach on their feet, thus utilizing proximity. They engage learners personally, hold high expectations of learners, and should not limit learners to grade level or perceived ability.

16. Educators and learners employ effective interpersonal communications skills.

17. Educators and learners celebrate the successes of others.

Core of Character Development

Great Expectations guides educators in modeling and teaching Life Principles at every grade level. Adherence to these fundamental virtues helps fulfill all that might be wished to be accomplished through character education. Students have the long-range benefit of attaining qualities that will serve them well in their personal and professional relationships for their whole lives.

Teachers may utilize the rich array of resources on the Great Expectations website, all of which are tailored to help teachers instill these valued characteristics in students.

Life Principles

Citizenship:	behaving in a responsible manner as a citizen of a community
Commitment:	keeping a promise or a pledge
Common Sense:	thinking before acting; using good judgment
Compassion:	ability to share another's feelings or ideas
Cooperation:	working together
Courage:	strength to act even when afraid or uncertain
Courtesy:	consideration, cooperation, and generosity
Dedication:	binding oneself to a course of action

Effort:	doing one's best in an endeavor
Empathy:	capacity for participating in another's feelings or ideas
Esprit de corps:	devotion among members of group for each other and the group's purpose
Flexibility:	ability to make adjustments or alter plans
Forgiveness:	act of forgiving for an offense; pardoning
Fortitude:	strength of mind that enables a person to encounter danger or bear pain or adversity with courage
Friendship:	caring for and trusting others
Honesty:	truthfulness
Humanitarianism:	promotion of human welfare and social reform
Humility:	being humble, not proud or haughty, not arrogant or assertive
Initiative:	taking action; originating new ideas
Integrity:	acting according to a sense of right and wrong
Justice:	being fair and upholding what is right
Loyalty:	faithfulness to another

Optimism:	an inclination to put the most favorable construction upon actions and happenings or to anticipate the best possible outcome
Patience:	enduring hardship, difficulty, or inconvenience with self-control
Patriotism:	love for or devotion to one's country
Perseverance:	ability to persist or continue striving to the end
Problem-Solving:	creating solutions; finding answers
Propriety:	standard of what is socially acceptable in conduct or speech
Resiliency:	recovering from or adjusting easily to misfortune or change
Respect:	paying proper attention or showing consideration to others
Responsibility:	making the choice to be reliable and dependable
Self-Discipline:	the ability to choose and control one's own actions
Service:	giving of one's time and energies to help others
Sincerity:	honesty of mind; freedom from hypocrisy
Temperance:	moderation in action, thought, or feeling

Great Expectations serves well in many settings: small rural schools, large metropolitan institutions, schools where students come from underprivileged homes, and others where students' families live in affluence. The GE methodology benefits students who are seeking to achieve ever higher levels of accomplishment and also students with learning disability struggles. Also it is in use at all grade levels from elementary through high school.

Students in GE schools are challenged to think creatively and to be problem solvers. They are asked to use higher-order thinking skills and to rise up to high expectations.

There is Bully Prevention at GE schools, but it happens because respect for others is woven into the fabric of the educational setting from the earliest days of a student's time at school. They are enveloped in a culture in which students are taught to show respect and to support and celebrate one another. Concerns about children being bullied are not handled by a separate discussion or day of training, but they are covered through the development of the appropriate school culture. It is a systemic approach; proper treatment of classmates is incorporated in every day. Students might say, "Becoming a good citizen is part of who we are."

All stakeholders in GE schools are pleased by the tangible effects of increased attendance, significantly reduced discipline referrals, and improved academic performance across the student body.

Great Expectations is a beautiful weave of the best practices in teaching, colored by ongoing research in education, and bearing accents of high standards of character. It is all made a reality in schools through invigorating training sessions for educators and encouraging advisement from coaches.

It is a way of life which leads to rich academic excellence and a spirit-sustaining culture of respect.

Substantiating Research on GE Effectiveness

Does the adoption of Great Expectations teaching methodology help students to perform academically at a higher plateau? Does it improve day-to-day teaching practice? Does it produce students who exhibit better conduct and improve their attendance? Are students in a Great Expectations classroom more likely to be interested and excited about school? Do parents observe positive responses in children whose teachers use Great Expectations practices? A growing body of research validates the power of Great Expectations, and answers these questions in the affirmative. Documents elaborating on these findings can be found on the GE Website.
<www.greatexpectations.org>

The K20 Center for Educational and Community Renewal is a statewide research and development center located on the research campus of the University of Oklahoma. This K20 Research Center designed a longitudinal quasi-experimental study which was completed in May of 2015. Findings showed that the GE Model Schools* had a higher mean passing rate than non-GE schools in both reading and math. This high mean passing rate was attained despite higher student to teacher ratios, higher teacher to administrator ratios, larger special education populations, and lower rates of spending for instruction. (*GE Model Schools are schools where 90% of the staff is implementing 100% of the Great Expectations Classroom Practices daily.)

Additionally, the cross-sectional view of school performance provided by the K20 Research Center demonstrated that GE Model Schools consistently attain higher pass rates year by year compared to other Oklahoma public schools. This type of positive descriptive comparison shows that GE Model Schools can potentially influence growth in achievement.

Oklahoma City Public Schools (OKCPS) released a **Research Study** in 2013 based on student performance on the Gates-MacGinitie Reading Test. It was a Matched Cohort Groups Reading Achievement Analysis of OKCPS GE Model School Cohorts compared to regular OKCPS Cohorts. Each student from the GE Model Schools and the traditional OKCPS Cohorts were matched on seven demographic indicators and also on the "pre-score" assessment score. The matched pairs showed that the GE Model School students outperformed the students from the OKCPS traditional schools at a statistically significant level.

The comparison of behavior data also showed that the GE Model Cohorts had much lower averages of discipline referrals and of short-term suspensions and fewer than half the total long-term suspensions of the traditional OKCPS cohorts. Furthermore, the GE Model Schools had higher attendance rates than the other OKCPS schools.

A **Study from the University of Oklahoma E-Team**, completed in 2004, found that "GE students made significantly higher gains than did non-GE students on nine out of ten available TerraNova scores." The findings indicate that students in classrooms implementing GE Methodology showed greater gains in student academic achievement during the school year compared to demographically similar students not exposed to GE. Other significant findings came from principal, teacher, parent, and student surveys and from classroom observations. The fact that parents noticed differences in their children's behavior indicates that the skills students learn in GE classrooms are also being used outside the classroom. Parents of students in Great Expectations class settings were significantly more likely to report that their children show interest, excitement, and involvement in learning and pleasure in learning activities. This is consistent with teacher and principal self-reports as well as observer ratings of classroom behavior. It is clear from this study that GE not only increases student achievement, but it also creates positive attitudinal and behavioral changes for principals, teachers, and students.

Great Expectations 17 Classroom Practices are the operational components of GE. Each practice has a compelling body of **Research Citations** that speak to its importance. GE teachers are expected to implement all 17 of these practices. A document on the Great Expectations website elaborates on the research and scholarly insight and advisement for each practice. See<http://www.greatexpectations.org/Websites/greatexpectations/images/pdf/Rationale_for_17_Practices.pdf>

A **"Crosswalk" Table of Three Models for Teacher Evaluation** (Marzano Teacher Evaluation Model, Danielson Framework for Teaching, and Tulsa Model for Observation and Evaluation) clearly demonstrates that a teacher who fully implements the 17 GE Classroom Practices will fulfill components of any one of these three models.

The **Southwest Educational Development Laboratory (SEDL)** in Austin, Texas, conducted a **Comprehensive Year-Long Research Study of Great Expectations**. They found that GE is unique nationally as a school reform model because GE combines best practices of good teaching with the teaching of social skills. Their findings showed GE elements substantially influence positive changes in classroom practices: creating active, interesting, hands-on lessons that integrate multiple subjects and have real-world connections; providing opportunities for students to work in small groups to complete projects; providing clear classroom expectations; establishing positive student-centered dialogues through which students' perspectives are considered and valued; giving students opportunities to have personal input and choices; and teaching life principles to students as well as facilitating student-to-student dialogues that help them learn social competence and social problem-solving skills. This longitudinal study, following third and seventh grade students, showed increased levels of achievement following the onset of GE implementation (62% of 3rd graders, 80% of seventh graders).

Harvard researcher, Dr. Ron Ferguson, conducted a study with 350 Oklahoma City Public School elementary teachers who attended a GE Winter Institute in January of 2011. A pre-training online survey, post-training online survey, and an end-of-the-semester online survey indicated that the GE Institute had a powerful impact on the belief and the actual classroom practices of these teachers.

Two separate studies, published as the following: ***Oklahoma Best Practices, What Works in High Challenge Elementary Schools*** (2005) and ***Oklahoma Best Practices, What Works in High Challenge Middle Schools*** (2006), looked at schools that consistently maintained average or above average test results in spite of operating under difficult circumstances (low income, varied ethnicity, and limited English proficiency). One of the conditions identified in both of these studies as a strong component benefiting the high challenge – high performing schools was the involvement of the staff in the Great Expectations practices.

"Given the political climate where educators are faced with greater demands for rigor, ever changing curriculum, and fewer resources, GE has been the cornerstone in assisting our staff in keeping everything 'pulled together.' With GE as our foundation, we can do whatever it takes to educate our children and to be able to give them important tools in life that will carry over into their adulthood. Rich, rigorous academic training is critical for our future generation – and it must be accompanied with quality of character. GE leads us in both areas!"
CHERYL LIDIA
Choctaw Elementary Principal, Choctaw, Oklahoma

Voices from Great Expectations Schools

To learn more directly how Great Expectations transitions from the statements of Tenets, the listing of Practices, the declaration of Expectations, and the expression of Life Principles, one can consider the case studies that follow. They include reports from a limited number, but widely diversified set of schools where GE is implemented to the level of GE Model School status. The summaries, based on interviews, provide a snapshot of what one might glean in visits to the schools or from personal conversations with these administrators.

How has Great Expectations impacted these schools? What difference has it made to teachers? What are the observable markers of academic and cultural improvements? The following statements answer those questions.

Affirmed and amazed by the possibilities

Lisa Moore, Principal
Plainview Elementary, Ardmore, Oklahoma
Rural GE Model School

Lisa Moore, the principal at Plainview Elementary, a rural school outside Ardmore, Oklahoma, is a huge fan of Great Expectations. When she took over the leadership of the school educating pre-kindergarten through second grade students, she and her teachers were doing everything they knew to do to raise achievement and create a good learning environment. As the school days progressed, things did not seem to be going well. Moore began to question herself, "Maybe my thinking is not correct. Maybe I don't know how to treat children and to guide teachers in coaxing best effort and proper attitudes from students."

Things changed when a friend invited Moore to attend a Great Expectations Summer Institute. She came away from the week feeling affirmed and amazed by the possibilities. She returned to school "on fire" with excitement for the vision she had gained for what should be happening in classrooms at Plainview.

Next, Ms. Moore invited a small nucleus of teachers to attend GE training, and then with their new understanding of GE Methodology, they returned and began implementing what they had learned. There was a truly impressive difference to be observed in the classrooms where teachers were applying the GE Classroom Practices, calling on students to live up to the Eight Expectations, and, they themselves, adhering to the Teachers' Creed.

The next plateau for Plainview came when all teachers attended training. Ms. Moore says, "That's when the transformation really happened!" The whole school became an extremely positive place; teachers loved coming to work. Plainview Elementary was a great place to be. The school-wide approach made the implementation especially powerful. Teachers shared ideas and observed one another in a generous, collegial manner. Old remnants of distrust and negativity disappeared.

There were other tangible changes. Attendance rose because children wanted to come to school. Test scores improved significantly. At the time that Plainview made the transition to being a GE school, the standardized test in use was the Iowa test. Before Great Expectations, the majority of students scored in the 70th percentile. Within a couple of years of full GE implementation, student scores were in the upper 90s. Principal Moore felt assured that teachers were using effective instructional practices. She and the whole school family were pleased by the dramatic improvement in test scores and in attendance. "There is an impressive magnitude in the growth in kids when everyone is doing the same thing," says Moore.

Parents were well satisfied by the changes at school. Ms. Moore especially appreciated the response of parents who were new to the community. She collected the comment from one move-in mom and dad who said, "When we walk into the building, we can tell a difference!"

Ms. Moore continues to be impressed by the power of the character-building that GE gives to the school. She says, "If you lose something, there are 'no worries,' because someone will return the misplaced object when it is found." She is pleased by the way discipline changed for her and the teachers. Students are given the avenue of assuming responsibility for their actions rather than undergoing punitive measures dictated for misconduct. Some Plainview children live in "tough" circumstances, but the commitment to developing life principles and applying quotations as reminders has helped all students grow toward being people of good character. For the troubled children with real difficulties to overcome, teachers are able to provide the coping tools they need.

Plainview Elementary has maintained status as a Model GE School for a number of years. If there is need to add a new teacher, the new hire must be GE trained. Ms. Moore's question of applicants is, "How much GE experience do you have?" She is building a staff of dedicated implementers, and teachers who join the school team are delighted to be part of the faculty of a school where Great Expectations is fully implemented.

Ms. Moore is genuinely enthusiastic about her role as principal. She benefits from the tips and feedback from the GE Instructional Coach, who visits the school. Moore says, "It is an advantage to have other schools come observe us as a Model School. Each time another school comes to watch our teachers in action, it raises our own awareness, and it is an encouragement to put out the best for company. Then it is wonderful to receive the positive comments and compliments. We love the affirmations for what the school is doing!"

Every great training is wrapped up in one package

Julie Altom, Principal
Plainview Intermediate, Ardmore, Oklahoma
Rural GE Model School

Plainview Intermediate, a school serving grades 3-5, is guided by Principal Julie Altom. Ms. Altom began her comments by speaking about attending GE training. She said, "Prior to coming to Plainview and being introduced to Great Expectations, I spent 18 years working in six other districts including two that were in other states. Within each district I had good training, but when I came to Plainview, I discovered that every good, or even great, training I had received previously was all wrapped up into one package in Great Expectations." She adds that she especially appreciates the research on best practices in teaching and the information on brain research in education that is presented in GE training sessions.

After teachers attended GE training, Principal Altom could clearly observe positive changes. She definitely appreciates the greater focus on guiding students in utilizing critical thinking because those higher-order thinking skills set students up for success through their whole school careers.

Additionally, the guidance from a GE Coach is a particular boon to the workings of the school and the rich implementation of Great Expectations. Ms. Altom remarks that the Instructional Coach assigned to Plainview has been particularly helpful in introducing valuable pointers to help teachers and in assisting the principal in her focus as she leads the school.

Other noteworthy aspects of school with Great Expectations as mentioned by Ms. Altom are, first of all, the difference when students are taught to speak in complete sentences. She observes that students are able to cement their thoughts on topics of discussion when they express themselves with full-length statements rather than one word answers. Furthermore, the

Eight Expectations provide teachers and principals an excellent tool for calling students to a high standard of behavior. If there is ever less-than-best conduct, then the student is asked to reflect on how his behavior measured up to the Eight Expectations. Teachers can keep the conversation positive, and students can take responsibility for their own actions and attitudes.

Ms. Altom also notes the fact that there is an "overflow of Great Expectations" beyond the walls of the school. The school shares the Life Principle word of the week, and parents take notice. Discussion and application of those components of good character bleed over into family life.

Altom is also able to quote impressive numbers to quantify the impact of Great Expectations at her school. There was a reduction in the number of office disciplinary referrals of 107 incidents from one year to only 40 incidents the following year. During the same period, suspensions dropped from 14 to only 3.

Grades and tests scores also speak to the effectiveness of Great Expectations teaching methodology. The percentage of students scoring advance or proficient in reading and math rose at every grade level by at least 1% and in some categories by as much as an impressive 11%.

The school report card overall grade raised from 89 (B+) to 93 (A). The Student Performance/Performance Index rose by a point or two in Reading and Math, and Student Growth for Math changed from an assessment of 87 (B) to 91 (A). The figures for the Bottom Quartile show Reading rising from 71 (C) to 75 (C) while Math improved from 59 (F) to 71 (C). Overall the ranking for the Bottom Quartile climbed from a D to a C.

Clearly, the school report data shows beneficial trends for students, and Principal Altom concludes, "I love the tools that GE provides to administrators, teachers, and students."

Building a skyscraper

Margaret Saunders Simpson, Principal
Andrew Johnson Elementary, Oklahoma City, Oklahoma
City GE Model School

In years past, before adoption of Great Expectations, Johnson Elementary did not function smoothly. There were no hallway procedures; at dismissal time, children charged out of the school with no exercise of courtesy. It was chaotic and not as safe as it needed to be. Exchanges between teachers and students were sometimes loaded with aggravation on both sides. Children were coming to the school building; but they were not being schooled in proper conduct, nor were they learning effectively.

When a principal who was well acquainted with Great Expectations took over the reins of the school, her influence laid the foundation for changes and for establishing an environment for learning. From that start, teachers attended GE training, Margaret Simpson moved into the principal role, and soon the school was not only implementing Great Expectations, but they were doing so at such an effective level that they were named a GE Model School. Now, the school continues to move forward with aspirations for ongoing growth. Simpson calls it "building a skyscraper on the foundation we have laid."

Especially valued by all stakeholders at the school is the family atmosphere that exists. Teachers and students treat one another with respect; and students, parents, and teachers, all know what to expect. The changes have been achieved through Great Expectations. Simpson refers to the implementation of the GE practices simply as the definition of how things work at Johnson. "Students and teachers speak in complete sentences, address one another by name, follow best practices, and learn enriched vocabulary," she says. "We hold high expectations for ourselves and the students."

One child who was new to the school told Principal Simpson, "I love Jaguar Jamboree!" That daily event is an all-school gathering named after the school mascot. The students participate in flag salutes, announcements, discussions of the word of the day, and recitations. The camaraderie with classmates and the enthusiasm for the school's focus on essential guidelines made the short assembly so powerful in the life of the new student that she insisted her parents help her always to be on time for that portion of the day.

Andrew Johnson Elementary is one of Oklahoma City's Great Expectations Model Schools. Recently, data was collected to compare the 24 Model Schools with 31 non-GE schools in the Oklahoma City District. The Model Schools compared with non-GE schools had 71% fewer office referrals, 70% fewer school suspensions, and 66% fewer absences from school. A review of the data shows that even the teachers at GE Model Schools had higher attendance. At the non-GE Schools, teachers' average attendance rate was 93.75% of the time while Model School teachers attended school and their teaching obligations 94.45% of the time.

Simpson concludes, "Great Expectations teaches the love of learning and enables the teachers themselves to be lifelong learners. The school is a family; teachers and students alike identify themselves as the school. We are Johnson."

Nighthawks SOAR

Christa Ellis, Principal
John Ross Elementary, Edmond, Oklahoma
Suburban GE Model School

Over an eleven year stint at John Ross, first as an assistant principal and now as the principal, Christa Ellis has enjoyed watching the large school's population of over 850 students and more than 95 staff members grow steadily into a family through the working of Great Expectations.

One activity that has brought about a greater sense of community at the school is the daily Rise and Shine Assembly. The time is a "call to excellence" with attention to expectations, patriotic songs, and occasions for showcasing students. It has proved to be an excellent opportunity for including parents and families in the high standards of the school's workday. One chant that students and teachers use as a frequent reminder is "Nighthawks SOAR!" The school mascot is the nighthawk, and the word SOAR is a quick acronym to keep the GE Eight Expectations on the tip of everyone's tongue:

S - STAY SAFE:
We will practice virtuous living using the Life Principles.
O - OWN YOUR OWN BEHAVIOR:
We will not laugh at or make fun of a person's mistakes, use sarcasm, or putdowns.
We will use good manners, saying, "please," "thank you," and "excuse me" and allow others to go first.
A - ACCEPT RESPONSIBILITY:
We will cheer each other to success.
We will help each other whenever possible.
R – RESPECT RELATIONSHIPS:
We will value one another as unique and special individuals.
We will recognize every effort and applaud it.
We will encourage each other to do our best.

Principal Ellis remarks how Great Expectations has helped to change the old school model of teachers in authoritative roles into the goal of teaching students how to function appropriately. Pupils need not always agree, but they do need to become attuned to treating others with respect and dignity.

As far as scholastic endeavors are concerned, John Ross Elementary is dedicated to constantly helping students grow.

GE helps promote academic excellence. Mrs. Ellis states that educators have shifted from the approach of standing up, delivering a lesson, and then considering the job done, to the strategy of helping students get what they need to learn successfully.

Enriched vocabulary is part of every classroom. Ellis especially delights in the vocabulary mastery of the youngest students; sometimes she is taken aback and thinks, "Did that comment just come out of the mouth of that small youngster?"

The faculty has a leadership team for GE that watches the implementation within the school. They have procedures in place to help every school day go smoothly. When a need arises for a new procedure, then the team carefully crafts the process to be followed. The Safety Patrol, manned by students, provides an opportunity for the fifth grade participants not only to carry out a helpful responsibility, but also to develop the capability of devising and reviewing the procedures the patrol is to use. It is an opportunity for them to develop skills that will truly serve them in the future.

The components of Great Expectations are interwoven in all the matters of school every day on the campus of John Ross Elementary.

GE is the common language

Ryan Huff, Principal
Central Middle School, Bartlesville, Oklahoma
Part of District-Wide Model GE School

Though Ryan Huff has been the principal at Central Middle School for nine years, Great Expectations has been a part of the school's methodology for only the last seven of those years. It has given Huff a clear view of how, in his words, "the culture of the school is totally different today because of GE."

The trend of improvement continues even after seven years. Mr. Huff cites the low tally of school suspensions. In the school year 2012-13, there were only 36 suspensions for the student body numbering over 700, and even better, in 2014-15, there were only 25.

At the beginning of Huff's tenure, there had been several turnovers of administrators. He could see that he needed to set the path for the school to follow. There were excellent teachers, but the overall climate of the school was not good. After the opportunity for teachers to attend Great Expectations Methodology training, the culture changed. Now there is a warm and welcoming environment. Both teachers and students stand ready to welcome guests to the school. There is more evidence of the culture in classrooms in the way students learn and even in the way they speak.

Although the school holds a mixture of students with widely differing socio-economic status, classmates have an appreciation for one another. Students set their sights on what they want to do and what they want to be and then are willing to reach out and help one another.

When Great Expectations started, it was first known to have an elementary application; and some older students were reluctant to take part in some of the procedures. However, once the classroom practices were deployed at the middle school, it became clear that GE is not just for the elementary setting. In fact, Bartlesville is now a Model District. Great Expectations is the common language for Pre-K students all the way through to seniors.

Besides the improved culture, the middle school students are prospering on test scores, and they especially profit from the GE Practice that critical thinking skills are taught. At Central Middle School, students enjoy the benefit of $60,000 from the Oklahoma Educational Technology Trust that allowed the purchase of a generous number of mini tablet computers.

These computers especially allow for assignments which relate class subject matter to the real world. Students collaborate, communicate, and produce quality work.

Huff also sees a great benefit from GE to parents as well as to students. It has enhanced the way he speaks with parents and finds that it helps him build a mutual respect. There are teams at the school that serve students if they have academic or personal issues, and some parents who historically have not had good experiences with schools come to know that teachers care and want their child to succeed. Visitors to the school are amazed at the great things going on.

Huff' says, "GE has been wonderful for our school."

GE enables teachers to redeem the time

Dr. Gary Quinn, Superintendent
Bartlesville Public Schools, Bartlesville, Oklahoma
District-Wide Model GE School

Dr. Quinn's assessment of Great Expectations includes the conclusion that the foremost benefit of GE is that it helps create the best possible atmosphere for learning. He says, "At Bartlesville, we believe we need a culture where there is respect and trust student to teacher and also student to student." Quinn observes that the positive learning environment helps teachers start class and have students on task without extraneous discussions stemming from problems or confusion over expectations.

Bartlesville values the learning strategies which teachers can utilize in their classrooms. Dr. Quinn has an eye on the clock for each school day. He believes GE enables teachers to redeem the time in the classroom. Time is so limited for teaching and learning, but if moments of the day are maximized, then teachers are able to help all students even those who need a little longer. And with Great Expectations, Bartlesville school sites all consistently report an attendance rate of 95%. Dropout rates at the upper level schools are low; all report less than 5% of the student population drops out of school. These figures mesh with Dr. Quinn's appreciation for redeeming the time. If students attend school and stay in school, they boost their learning opportunities.

A further attribute of Great Expectations, according to Quinn, is the benefit it provides to administrators; it helps principals develop their own personal capacity to be educational leaders. They learn what to ask of their teachers for quality instruction, and they learn to fill the crucial role of being guides for teachers and students. Great Expectations Leadership Training has helped principals develop that crucial capability.

Dr. Quinn speaks with enthusiasm of the fact that the whole community of Bartlesville has embraced GE. Billboards around town feature the Great Expectations Life Principles. The local chamber of commerce and United Way promote the word of the month. In his monthly local radio program, Dr. Quinn has the opportunity to prompt parents to do their part in discussing, developing, and reviewing the word of the month in their homes.

As an administrator, Dr. Quinn must be concerned with keeping the faculty up to speed with Great Expectations. When new teachers are added to the school's staff, they are given the opportunity to attend GE training during the summer so they have had training before the school year starts. Quinn welcomes the positive comments that come back to him from teachers, and he enjoys the fact that teachers really value GE.

Dr. Quinn remembers Charlie Hollar, the founder of Great Expectations. That memory is accompanied by a true appreciation for Charlie and his vision. Dr. Quinn says, "Great Expectations is a great gem, and we are fortunate to have such quality training available right here in our state."

The 17 Practices are a good checklist for everyone

Chris Nester, Principal
Teachers: Lori Moore, Cricket Roberts, and Cathryn Sutton
Coppell Wilson Elementary School, Coppell, Texas
Texas GE Model School

The main area that Chris Nester thinks of first with regard to Great Expectations is the unified vision it affords the school. All of the faculty and staff are on the same page for the day-to-day operation of classes, routines, and plans. He applauds the comfort level available to teachers by their knowing what's expected of them and their students. If the school has goals, stakeholders are easily able to speak the same language in laying out the action steps to reach the desired objectives.

Nester also appreciates, as an administrator, the profile of a teacher placed in his mind because of the definition of GE best practices. A teacher who is not yet following Great Expectations Tenets is quickly identifiable. Then as the school leader, he knows he needs to help that teacher make adjustments if he or she plans to continue at the school.

Wilson Elementary is part of the overall high-performing Coppell School District. Although Wilson has a high ratio of economically disadvantaged students as well as young people for whom English is a second language, the school has still been able to show incremental improvements each year. In addition to the climbing test scores, Mr. Nester values the social and emotional well-being of students because the teachers "love the kids."

The school doesn't use a system of office referrals. Nester doesn't track any such problem, and the teachers don't have referral forms to use. Rather, the principal is kept advised of any student who is in need of help early on before behavior mistakes become a real problem. The approach is to look for what is causing problems and turn the situation into a learning opportunity for the child rather than making it a call for punitive action. Well past the middle of the school year, Mr. Nester reported that there had been no in-school suspensions at all during the year.

Any time Wilson welcomes visitors into the building, those guests are truly impressed by the children's behavior. Also, Mr. Nester has learned that substitute teachers gladly sign up for repeat duty at his school site because they know the students will be ideally cooperative and respectful.

Lori Moore, a Wilson PE teacher, loves the impact of GE on the school. She's glad for the common language for all classrooms. School-wide, teachers and students refer to the quotation of the week, the poem for recitation, or the newest callback.

First grade teacher Cathryn Sutton thinks initially of how the culture of the school has changed dramatically. The whole school has become a family with students who have more choices and are more likely to initiate learning and best behavior.

Cricket Roberts treasures the good manners and the understanding of how to respond to adults that have become second nature to the Wilson third grade students she teaches. She tells of the experience of attending a district middle school awards ceremony. It had been customary in the past for students to drag across the stage to pick up whatever certificate they were being awarded. Their demeanor was self-conscious with no eye contact or verbal response to the presenters. But as Roberts watched and especially noted any young people who had previously been at Wilson with all of the Great Expectations instructions about employing effective interpersonal communications skill, she was proud to note that every young person who had been a Wilson student carried himself with obvious pride, shook the hands of the presenters, and gave eye contact. The display of poise had become ingrained in those young people, and that competence will be a personal capability which will serve those individuals their whole lives.

The Wilson teachers agree that the 17 Classroom Practices are a good checklist for teachers to use to evaluate themselves, and all the Wilson educators use the practices for providing feedback to one another. They have instituted what they call "Pop and Post." One teacher will pop into another teacher's classroom unannounced. The visiting teacher will be on the lookout for evidence of the four or five highlighted practices of the week, and then that visitor will leave a post-it note with feedback on observations. The teachers are given valuable affirmations and occasionally some beneficial help and encouragement.

Students also get some feedback on ways they embrace the life principles. When the school first shifted to Great Expectations, the teachers were truly concerned about what would happen if they discontinued their custom of using rewards, giving out tokens, or getting students to accumulate some tangible marker for good conduct. As it turns out, those tangible rewards are now a thing of the past, and they are not missed. Students have the intrinsic motivation to be good citizens, and they understand the life principles. The school celebrates, in a number of ways, when the various members of the student body demonstrate the true meaning of the targeted character traits by their conduct.

A framework of how to do business

Dr. Maricela Helm, Principal
Amy Parks Elementary, Rockwall, Texas
Texas GE Model School

Amy Parks Elementary is a Model School even though it is only the third year of GE implementation for them. To start with, the recommendation for Great Expectations training first came from a parent who had a sister using GE in Oklahoma.

Actually, the school had tried a number of education programs and already had several in place. However, a survey of parents revealed there were some families who said their child did not feel welcome at school, and some had issues with peers. As the school leadership began looking at bullying programs, the same mom again suggested Great Expectations as a beneficial plan to help the school.

A teacher team went to GE Summer Institute to gather information. Principal Helm received a call after the first day with the report that "This is not really about bullying." The teacher who called reported, "GE is about building a culture of respect, teaching problem-solving, holding high expectations, modeling excellent character...." Then she added, "I guess if we could do all that, then bullying would not be a problem."

The school followed up by sending teachers to training, and the faculty members loved it. The whole staff was sold on GE. Now everyone who is to teach at Amy Parks attends Great Expectations training. In fact, discussion of GE is part of any job interview process. Teachers are told, "If you plan to teach here, then you will go to GE training."

Great Expectations gives the campus a framework of how to do business. The goals and standards trickle down to the students, and the community richly supports the school. Parents are models of the desired character traits and demonstrate how much they value service.

The school district considers some other programs and, in fact, institutes the application of some additional plans for every site in the district. Stephen Covey's *Seven Habits* is a good guide for building leadership skills. Dr. Robert Marzano's *Best Practices and Instructional Strategies* provides research-based, effective instructional strategies. But what Dr. Helm and her teachers have concluded is that aspects of such programs are built-in to GE, and any additional implementation efforts are perfectly aligned with GE. Great Expectations supports these additional efforts; all are connected because of GE's being research-based.

"GE has been a life saver," says Dr. Helm. Teachers usually struggle with new programs, additional things to handle, and changes. They think, "Oh, no, something new!" But instead, GE gives teachers freedom. They are allowed to approach new matters with the frame of mind that we are all learners, and mistakes are ok. GE has helped teachers grow and has built-in common sense. Everyone learns from mistakes, and all learn from each other. As they teach the children, GE is also teaching teachers.

GE has its challenges because there are many aspects of what all should be happening at a school, but it also builds a foundation. Teachers develop the sense that they can handle all the facets of establishing a culture for learning and helping students achieve academic excellence.

Dr. Helm says, "At our school, the implementation of Great Expectations has become seamless. We don't stop and do GE; it is a part of what we do all the time, every day."

We steal from students if we don't give them this experience

Erin Sullivan, Principal
Bay-Arenac Community High School, Essexville, Michigan
Michigan Model GE High School

Erin Sullivan, in her fifth year as principal of Bay-Arenac Community High School, says achieving GE Model status was a journey for the school. The school is an alternative high school. The students consider Bay-Arenac a second chance. In their past school careers, the students have had difficulties with poor attendance, bullying, or failing classes. The school has teenage students who are parents, many youth who have encountered issues with the court system, and several who just did not fit in at the more traditional and much larger high schools. As Sullivan began her leadership role, she could see places where the school was struggling. The overarching problem was a lack of student respect for teachers, for the school facility, and, in fact, even for themselves. Faculty meetings were spent discussing discipline needs. When Great Expectations was explained and presented to the teachers, they were ready to consider GE training and the changes it could bring.

Sullivan says that of all the school reforms, GE made the most sense to them. She remarks that, in general, teachers learn best practices in their preliminary teacher training, but then when facing all the student issues and the hectic pressures inherent in the role of teaching, educators forget to do the things they learned.

Community High School moved forward with training for everyone including support staff and non-certified school liaisons. They have worked hard and now continue to strive for implementation of 100% of the practices daily. With the advisement of the GE teams which are a part of the school faculty, they all keep stretching for deeper and richer application of the practices and for true assimilation of the Life Principles. Teachers and staff use the Eight Expectations to redirect any student who is out of step with proper behavior. Principal Sullivan enjoys hearing affirmations, words of encouragement, and frequent congratulations between teachers and students. She says that the school has adapted celebrations to best fit the culture of the school.

There are a number of innovative ways this high school is fulfilling the GE Practices:

- They have converted the hallways to art galleries with postings of famous artists' work, biographies on each artist, and student art work that emulates the well-known art pieces. Educators are teaching just by the postings in the hallways.
- Additionally, student work is displayed in the hallways. All staff members make sure they walk through to look at the displays and use sticky notes to add feedback.
- Students are in charge of displaying information about the Eight Expectations on windows and glass showcases. Students take ownership in promoting the expectations, and there is a different feel to the process because it is student-led.
- Students display their written personal goals, and then they can enjoy celebrating with classmates when they reach their objectives. This process is called SWAG for "Student Who Achieves Goals." SWAG successes are honored at "Bulldog Blitz," the regular all-school assembly.
- Daily announcements presented by students on the public address system are another leadership-development opportunity. Students are glad to take turns presenting the creed, a word of the week, the quotation of the day, and various announcements. Students develop personal communication skills and gain experience with a public address system at the same time.
- The school builds in enrichment through field trips for students whose family economic background limits what they have experienced. The outings are not only enjoyable, but they also demand of students that they live up to high expectations for their behavior.

Principal Sullivan reports the good benefits of a recent midyear celebration day. Because of the entry level of accomplishment for the student population, it is noteworthy that two students earned all A's, and several had perfect attendance. Sixty percent of the students had passing grades; some of those students had not had passing grades since fourth grade, so the group enjoyed honoring one another. One student actually completed all coursework to graduate at the midyear point. He was called to the front and received acknowledgement, a diploma, and a pin. He returned to his seat, smiling and waving that coveted piece of paper. Others in the student body saw that graduation can be within reach. Sullivan says, "Classmates think, 'I want that, too!'" The students become an inspiration for one another, and they start attending tutoring and knuckle down to complete assignments.

Over the past three to four years, Bay-Arenac Community High School has had a notable increase in the graduation rate and a decrease in the drop-out rate. It has been steadily improving each year. There has been a significant increase in the school's retention rate; that is, the number of students who stick with schooling for their whole high school career. The number of students who remain on the roster through the end of the school year has almost doubled from its pre-GE figure. For the past two years, the honor roll list has averaged 20 students per quarter, an increase from the previous average of 14. Happily, Great Expectations has also had a positive impact on discipline. Sullivan says when she started at the school, there might be 5 to 7 expulsions that she would need to report to the school board at each meeting. Now her report is perhaps 3 expulsions, and during some reporting periods, there are no expulsions at all.

Great Expectations has been a most important help. It gives the staff consistency, and all talk the same language. At least for some teachers who had been shy students themselves, the practice of standing and speaking in complete sentences seemed, at first, to be asking too much. But the school is a safe environment in which to practice such an important life skill. Sullivan is adamant that students need speaking in formal register as preparation for job interviews or for opportunities in college classes. They need the competence to be articulate with peers and adults. She says, "We are giving students a gift when we make speaking before others the norm. We steal from students if we don't give them this experience!"

For Principal Sullivan herself, being a GE leader gives her license to encourage and to hold teachers accountable. She helps the whole school team see the great good, and she can readily say, "We are a GE school, so this is what we need to do." She relishes the times when visitors comment, "This school feels joyful when you walk in."

Her concluding thought is "Why wouldn't you want to be GE?"

Can see the striking need

Lonnie Moser, Principal
Chetopa Elementary School, Chetopa, Kansas
Rural Kansas GE Model School

With mostly secondary experience, Lonnie Moser shifted recently into the role of principal at Chetopa Elementary. He started his tenure by attending Great Expectations Summer Institute to learn about GE and become acquainted with ways he needed to help teachers maintain the school's Model School status. Working at the school with the goal of supporting the teachers, Moser soon realized that Great Expectations is exactly what it purports to be, a school transformation model. He comments, "It is bigger than other training programs. It changes a school's culture and becomes the way we do things."

Mr. Moser is in a position to observe the striking need for Great Expectations to be carried on up the scale to the junior high school. The contrast in culture between the elementary with Great Expectations and the junior high without is dramatic. He sees that the older students who are resistant to adults and unkind to one another seriously need the GE intervention of instilling kindness and consideration for others in their school days. They need to be trained by teachers whom they respect and who respect them.

Kim Pitner, the Great Expectations Coach, who works with Chetopa Elementary, has some additional insights about the workings of the school and the role that GE has played there. Tragically, the school lost its superintendent to cancer, and, added to that, there were also other administrative and faculty shifts. Focus on GE gave the school the consistency and positive attitude they needed to weather all the changes that swept over the school because of the turnover in staff and leadership.

The GE teachers focused on results and demanded consistency from one another. They were uplifted by the words of the school creed. They didn't just hold their ground, they moved forward. Chetopa Elementary School was awarded the Challenge Award of Recognition for accomplishment in closing the achievement gap in both Reading and Math at the fourth grade level based on the Kansas Assessment results. Additionally, the school has several classrooms which have received the Standard of Excellence Award from the Kansas Department of Education. In order to receive this award, a classroom must have at least 25% of their students score Exemplary (the highest performance level) and no more than 5% of their students score in Academic Warning (the lowest performance level). The teachers declare these awards are a result of the hard work of the entire elementary teaching staff and their dedication to the students of Chetopa Elementary.

In the tight-knit community, the teachers, who are steeped in Great Expectations, reach beyond the walls of their classrooms to do more for students and for the students' parents. They conduct an after-school program. The work with parents allows for building relationships and setting academic goals. The program promotes academics, makes sure students and their families have the resources they need, and gives parents pointers on how to help their children. The interaction is good for all concerned.

Pitner says, "The Chetopa teachers want to leave a legacy and to use the vehicle of the school to give kids a better life."

The tyranny of urgency crowds out the application of things learned in a one-day professional development session

Dr. Al King, Headmaster
Oklahoma Christian School, Edmond, Oklahoma
Parochial School

Dr. Al King, Headmaster at Oklahoma Christian School, thinks first of the comprehensive nature of Great Expectations training. He appreciates the two-pronged focus on teaching techniques as well as building students' character and polishing the culture of the school. He says, "If the culture is a failure, then other teaching is canceled or diminished."

His next point of value for GE is the great follow-up that is provided. For most professional development pieces, educators go to a workshop, but then they must implement without any support. King says, "The tyranny of urgency crowds out the application of things learned in a one-day professional development session, so such 'training' is not good use of time and energy." Its rich and varied means of on-going support make GE sustainable.

One piece of that support comes from the Great Expectations Coach, who acts as a consultant for Dr. King and the school's teachers. This Instructional Coach is a third party who comes to the school solely for the sake of helping teachers improve, not to evaluate. Teachers need not be "on guard" and can listen to recommendations, knowing that the comments are intended to help them enhance their teaching practices.

The funding through a GE grant has been invaluable to the school, and now Headmaster King is seeking additional training aimed specifically at the secondary level.

King says he can see a massive change since the adoption and application of Great Expectations Practices. Students are more polite, and discipline issues have gone down. GE has helped create a culture that is loving and kind. Education at Oklahoma Christian School is interwoven with Biblical teachings, and the school intends to promote passages like I Corinthians Chapter 13 which speaks of love. GE bonds with that intent and gives specific tools and ways for conducting oneself. There are concrete steps for exhibiting consideration for others, not just the admonition to "show respect."

Oklahoma Christian School provides education for classes pre-school through high school seniors, but the grade levels are housed in separate buildings. With such detachment, it is easy to lose continuity between levels, but for the headmaster and the 60 teachers at the school, GE gives common skills and a crucial cohesiveness.

If it is important, then we need to do it really well

Ken Willy, Headmaster
Oak Hall Episcopal School, Ardmore, Oklahoma
Parochial GE Model School

Headmaster Ken Willy is serving his third year at Oak Hall Episcopal School. It is his first position with a school where Great Expectations is applied, so he has the perspective of one coming from a school without GE to one with GE.

Oak Hall was the first private school in the country to become a GE Model School, and the institution continues to embrace GE. Willy says, "It makes a difference in the culture." He also remarks that Great Expectations and the faith focus of the school's program complement one another.

Willy points out the perspective of how wonderful GE is especially for new faculty members. It provides an umbrella of understanding for all whether an educator has twenty-five years experience or is a first-year teacher. The expectations are made clear for students, faculty, and staff. It helps a new teacher "get into the swing of things at a school." GE helps that new colleague to be able to interact with companion teachers and students on a level field.

Great Expectations provides stability across the board, not just in one classroom. Faculty at meetings and children in class know what to do and why. And there is great value to the fact that teachers and students build up one another and cheer each other to success.

Willy points out that the use of a phrase as a consistent callback signal makes wonderful common sense, and he appreciates the tactic of a respectful approach to a student who has made a poor choice. He has watched a teacher speak quietly to a student who has shown misconduct. The teacher asked the student to reflect on circumstances and then gave the child ownership of correcting his own behavior.

Headmaster Willy sees the value of GE for the consensus it gives all the school population of how to interact. His teachers love Great Expectations, and he continues to challenge teachers saying, "What do you do and why do you do it? If it is important, then we need to do it really well."

A cowboy code of conduct

Leah Mulkey, Education Coordinator
Chisholm Trail Heritage Center, Duncan, Oklahoma
GE Model Museum

The Chisholm Trail Heritage Center is a museum with the "goal of celebrating and perpetuating the history, art, and culture of the Chisholm Trail, the American Cowboy, and the American West." At first impression, a museum would not have need for the training and teaching strategies offered through Great Expectations, but this facility has been utilizing GE practices for a number of years and, in fact, has been named a Great Expectations Model School. Last year, 7,300 students, a record number of attendees, participated in museum classes.

Those many students arrive at the museum with the teachers from their home classrooms. The museum staff became interested in Great Expectations a number of years ago because they could tell when students walked in the front door if they came from a school where Great Expectations was being implemented. Education Coordinator Leah Mulkey recounts that there is a different feel with GE students. They know what conduct is expected, and they behave at a higher standard.

The sessions at the museum offer some valuable insights and enrichments which supplement lessons from the students' regular classrooms. The groups of children are at the museum for only four hours at the most, so the museum educators must maximize their time. They use a "cowboy code of conduct" rather than a creed. All the sessions are rich in vocabulary, and vocabulary words are generously posted around the facility. It is expedient for the museum teachers to use callbacks, just as the regular school teachers do, and critical thinking skills get much exercise because the children are asked to ponder many challenging queries during their time at the center.

One of the sections taught at the museum is "History Heroes on the Chisholm Trail." Its lessons underscore the understanding of the fact that people in the late 1800's had to be inventive. If there were problems with no solutions, then the cattlemen, trail drivers, and territory residents had to create solutions. The discussions in the museum sessions are a basis for helping children see the real world and to take home the concept of problem-solving. The museum instructors meet students at the door wearing period dress and model life principles throughout their interaction with the children.

The engaging activities at the museum, featuring not only arts and history, but also math, science, entrepreneurship, and much more, offer enrichment especially through some resources that are not available in a regular school classroom. There is a new art exhibit every eight weeks. One such exhibit features the artwork of George Catlin. Students learn about Catlin's artwork and his travels, then they have an opportunity to create their own Catlin-like landscape with chalk. They learn of foreground, background, horizon, and shading and are shown how to put a winding river in their scene to show depth just as Catlin might. They use mediums that are not available in their home classrooms, become familiar with art terms, and return home with work to be put on display.

The carefully planned activities make the museum time meaningful, and Mulkey states Great Expectations and the GE-trained faculty are the reason teachers return and bring students time and again. Of the schools which have come for the museum sessions, 98% of them return in subsequent years; this is truly an excellent retention rate.

There are many glowing comments given to the museum staff by teachers who have brought their classes to attend the instruction at the museum. For example, Linda Wilkerson, a 3rd Grade teacher from Marlow, Oklahoma, said, "It was a super learning experience! Even the teacher learned."

Section II
Great Expectations in Action

Prologue

Vicarious Visit

"A book is a version of the world."
SALMAN RUSHDIE

Great Expectations has a story, and now in this section we come to it. The early section of this book detailed the components of the GE teaching model based on research of what exactly are the best practices in teaching and carefully crafted with a delineation of the basic tenets which are the pillars supporting all the endeavors that flow from the assignment of providing education to learners.

With the matters of the Great Expectations Practices in mind as well as the enumeration of the Expectations and the noble elements of the Life Principles, readers can now forge forward into "The Story," and accept the challenge to identify the components of GE in action.

What follows is the account of a family moving to a new town. The offspring of the family have anxieties about being assimilated into the new school with the unknown aspects of teachers, classmates, and the social mores of life in a community where they are outsiders. Additionally, the telling of the events of the school year encompass the experiences not only of the single family of newcomers but also of the teachers and classmates whom they encounter as the school year unfolds.

The family, the first-year teacher, and all the other people whom you will meet in this story are fictional, but the experiences of Great Expectations – related as if they were part of the characters' lives – are all based on true happenings in actual GE classrooms and schools.

Read on for Great Expectations in action.

*"The more that you read,
the more things you will know.
The more that you learn,
the more places you'll go."*

DR. SEUSS

Chapter 1

New Year, New School, New Town

*"Still around the corner, there may wait,
a new road or secret gate."*
J.R.R. TOLKIEN

"One box less, one box less!" Those were the words running through Lyle Hanson's mind as he traveled for the umpteenth time the sixteen steps up and down the stairs leading to the bonus room in their new home. He was hauling the last of the boxes from the moving van, and he was sweating in the August heat. Also, his thoughts kept returning to the supervisor job he was to start on Monday. His biggest concern: would the members of his work team be people of integrity? He believed he could lead if the employees under his guidance would follow.

Lyle's other worry was for the quality of the local school system for his three children. He and his wife Julie had been assured repeatedly that the school system in Center City was excellent. In fact, the realtor who sold them the house had been effusive in his praise of the schools.

"All the school sites are Great Expectations schools," he said. When neither Lyle nor Julie responded to that comment, the realtor went on to say, "You do know about Great Expectations, don't you?"

"Well," said Lyle with a note of hesitation, "I remember a little about reading the Charles Dickens book when I was in high school."

"Oh, right," laughed the realtor, then he continued, "No, this Great Expectations is a way of teaching and, really, of conducting all school business and activities. I know about it because my wife is a teacher. She talks about it all the time. She was discouraged and ready to quit teaching. She was just flat not happy, but then things changed dramatically after she went to GE training."

"*GE* training?" said Julie. She didn't follow the realtor's comment.

"Oh, much of the time she says 'GE' instead of Great Expectations. After that first summer session, she rediscovered her excitement about teaching. She talks about the fact that Great Expectations is all based on research of the best practices in teaching. Her students are doing well academically, and best of all, the culture of the school makes it an encouraging place to work. Your kids will enjoy it."

Lyle's thoughts about the school system were interrupted by Julie's appearance with glasses of iced tea. He couldn't turn down the offer of a break and a cold drink. As they sat on the stairway under an air conditioning vent, he said, "Well, what do you think? Still believe we've made the right move?"

"It's all good," she said. The boxes Lyle had been carrying from the truck to the bonus room were her business inventory. Her personal "job" was combing garage sales, auctions, flea markets, and any other venue where she might purchase special small collectable items for resale at a profit online. Such an endeavor allowed her the flexibility to be an active supporter of her children's activities, and she appreciated the challenge of the accompanying research on the wide array of items she purchased. Though her response to Lyle's question was positive, in the back of her mind was a poignant wish for her children. Her own schooling had been so different from the educational experiences she had observed for her three children to date. Changing times had brought demands for high test scores, differences in the ways of society in general, frightening scenarios that made even elementary schools dangerous, a widening gap between affluence and poverty of families, and a decline of moral values. Her own school experience seemed as if it came from a different day and time. She and her classmates had enjoyed a sense of community and camaraderie, as well as pride in the school. She had received a good education but also a legacy of how to be a good citizen. None of those aspects had been a strong part of school life for the Hanson children in their educational settings so far. That made her sad. "Maybe in the new schools," she thought wistfully.

"Mom!" called the plaintive voice of Sarah, the Hansons' daughter, who would sign up for her senior year at Center City High School next Friday. "Where is my backpack?" Sarah was in her upstairs bedroom, shuffling through stacks of boxes.

Julie called back, "It is in a box in your room."

"Right," thought Sarah with dismay. Somehow the possessions that had been stored in her modestly-sized closet and dresser in the old house had exploded to fill a room with cardboard cartons. She had never been through the process of moving before, so when she followed her mother's directive to label all the boxes she packed, she had done so by writing "SARAH'S ROOM" on each box. Now she couldn't identify which box contained what!

Sarah was anxious. She was ready for her senior year and had thought she would share all the final high school year festivities in the comfort of a familiar setting with her well-known teachers and classmates. Instead, her family moved; now, she had apprehensions about completing her graduation requirements, applying for scholarships, and finding anyone she might call a friend at the new school. "I will be totally starting over to make friends! How will I even know where to sit in the cafeteria?" she thought.

Down in the garage, Gabe, Sarah's seventh grade brother, was supposed to be putting the sports equipment away in a cabinet. His mouth hurt from the braces that had just been applied to his teeth. He hurled his soccer cleats into the cabinet. The strength of that fling matched his angry mood. No soccer for him, just when he had worked his way up to being a starter on his team back home. Yes, Center City had soccer, but it was only in the spring and only at the high school and that left him out. He was much better at running and moving than sitting still in a classroom.

The next box Gabe opened had his soccer ball, shin pads, a football, Frisbees, and... the scooter he'd gotten as a birthday present three years ago. He eyed the sloping driveway; it might make a good scooter track. His feet had grown prodigiously, but he was able to crowd one foot onto the scooter platform.

"I'll just give it a short test run," he thought.

He went gliding down the drive and along the street. Yes! It was great for "scootering;" the box unpacking, the sore spots in his mouth from the rubbing braces, and all the expected tedium of a seventh grade classroom were momentarily forgotten.

Although Gabe was feeling more light-hearted with each foot shove to pump the scooter, Jackson, his brother who was soon-to-be a second grader, was near tears. He was sitting on the step at the back door, but he was alone. "Back home," he would have been joined by Big Gray and Callie when he stopped on the step to put on his outside shoes. The two were his special cat friends who'd been left behind when the family moved. Big Gray was a tomcat with soft gray fur and blue eyes that always seemed to have a wise look. Callie, a calico cat, was Big Gray's fun-loving, feisty female companion.

His parents had considered moving the cats, but they were strictly outdoor cats. Though the duo was devoted to Jackson, they were also staunch in their commitment to stick close to their home locale. Lyle and Julie's best guess was that the nearly feral felines would not stay put if they were hauled to a new residence. And, two wandering cats would most certainly have their lives in peril if they tried, on their own, to pick their way miles and miles back to familiar territory.

All the rationale for "what was best for the cats" had been explained to Jackson. However, now he had no furry friends who rushed to purr and lean in to him each time he came outside. The biggest ache came from his worry that the new people at the old house would not look after them, and he knew Big Gray and Callie didn't understand why their friend Jackson had abandoned them. "You can't explain things to a cat!" he grieved.

৵৵

While the moving-in process was going on at the Hansons' new residence, a near neighbor was experiencing some trepidation of her own about the start of the school year. It was Rachel Mullins, or Mrs. Mullins, as she would be addressed by her class of first graders. Rachel and her husband, Chad, were newlyweds, and her job at Lavonia Berber Elementary was her first full-time teaching assignment.

Rachel was already at the school building and in the midst of arranging her classroom. Other teachers from her hallway all seemed happy and excited about the start of the school term. Many had stepped into her room to welcome her.

She'd met with Principal Aransus, as part of her job interview. Rachel had been impressed with her cheerful manner and the excitement in her voice as she spoke about the upcoming school term. "Lavonia Berber Elementary is a Great Expectations school," Mrs. Aransus had explained, "and we will want you to become thoroughly acquainted with implementing the GE Practices."

Today, Mrs. Aransus had come to her room and handed her a notebook with GE materials: Pages on the 6 Basic Tenets, 17 Classroom Practices, 8 Expectations for Living, and 36 Life Principles.

"We have a morning assembly for about ten minutes of every day; it is a call to excellence for the students and the teachers as well," Mrs. Aransus said. "Come by my office; I have a page that outlines what you can expect for such an assembly; we call it 'Rise and Shine.'"

Then she smiled and pressed a card into Rachel's hand. It had a picture of a ship sailing out from a harbor, and bore the words: "A ship is safe in the harbor, but that's not what ships are for." Mrs. Aransus had written the additional message, "Good luck with the beginning of this special assignment of First Grade teacher! You are sailing to wonderful new horizons."

"The other teachers can help you with about anything you need. Our GE Coach will come and work with all of us. You can count on receiving some direct Great Expectations training soon, and please know that you can come to me with your questions." She gave Rachel a hug and hurried on to tackle other jobs on her list.

Rachel reread her card and then pinned it to the bulletin board behind her desk.

"Anchors aweigh!" she thought, "I am sailing out of the harbor into open seas!"

"Starting a new way is never easy so… keep starting until the start sticks."
TIM FARGO

Chapter 2

Expectations, Creeds, and Life Principles

"A spoonful of sugar helps the medicine go down."
MARY POPPINS

    A note from Principal Aransus peeked out of Rachel Mullins's mailbox in the teachers' lounge. It read, "Be sure to have two or three positive contacts with the parents of your students before Open House." Then Mrs. Aransus had drawn her own rough, but cute, sketch of Mary Poppins, including an umbrella with a parrot-head handle, a black boater hat decked with flowers, and a large carpet bag. Rachel flipped the page over, but it was blank on the back. She was still pondering the significance of the drawing when Mrs. Johnson came to check her mail.

    "Hi, Rachel, how are things going?" asked Mrs. Johnson.

    "Going great," she replied. It was always a treat to see Eve Johnson, an amiable second grade teacher. Rachel guessed that Eve would be the one able to explain the drawing on the principal's memo. "Is there some reason for this drawing?" she asked, holding out the page with the sketch of the magical English nanny.

    Eve glanced at the note as she gathered up her own mail. "That is Mary Poppins!" she said. "She is there to remind us that parents will be more receptive to our comments calling for their child's improvements when they have already gotten acquainted with us and built some trust and appreciation for how things are running here at school."

    "Ok, I get it now," murmured Rachel, half to herself. "If we have given some happy words, the reports that call for corrections will be more palatable. A spoonful of sugar helps the medicine go down."

Rachel thanked Mrs. Johnson and headed back to her classroom. It was almost time for her students to return from music class. Although it was still the first month of school, Rachel was pleased with how the term had started for her and her first grade students. The Great Expectations implementation was going more smoothly than she had expected because all of her colleagues were using the same terminology and calling on the students with the same expectations. Most of her first graders already knew the ropes of GE because of their experience as kindergarteners. The challenge for Rachel was to be consistent in adhering to the classroom procedures she had instituted herself during the first week of school.

For a lunch line procedure, Rachel asked students to stand in a queue, with no talking until the class member who was the leader for the day led them down the hall to the cafeteria. Nicholas, a talkative newcomer to the school, had not yet made a habit of standing silently, even though the wait was only two or three minutes long.

Rachel really liked the Great Expectations example of using quotations to reinforce requests for particular behaviors. To provide a good reminder to Nicholas and any of his classmates who were talking when they were supposed to be listening, she had prepared a poster featuring the American humorist Mark Twain and one of his quotations: "If we were meant to talk more than listen, we would have two mouths and one ear."

Today as they lined up for lunch, Nicholas had been full of comments and questions. Rachel moved along the line until she was near Nicholas; she thought it was worth trying close teacher proximity as a classroom management technique. Nicholas was still talking. She leaned over and looked him in the eye, and thinking of the quotation about listening more with two ears than talking with one mouth, she said, "Nicholas, what did Mark Twain say about talking and listening?"

Nicholas hardly missed a beat. His reply was "We should have two mouths!" That was not the response she expected, but she realized that from Nicholas's perspective, he had given the perfect analysis of the Twain quotation!

After a brief conversation with the whole class, in which some of Nicholas's classmates were able to elaborate on the more standard message of the Twain quote and review the classroom procedure of no talking during the lunch line-up, Rachel and the Mullins First Grade Squad filed down the hallway. On the way, Rachel spotted Eve Johnson standing at her classroom door, ready to lead her second graders to the lunch room right behind Rachel's First Graders. Since Rachel had seen Eve at the teacher mailboxes earlier in the day, Eve had undergone a bit of a transformation. She looked as if she had been doused with snowflakes. There was downy white fluff in her brown hair, on her eyelashes, and dotting her dark blouse.

When Rachel was able to ask Eve about all the white fluff that had been added to her hair and clothes, Eve replied, "Today was show and tell for my students. Did you know one fuzzy brown spike of the tall, reed-like marsh plant called cattail may contain a million tiny seeds! Each seed has a tuft of silky white hairs. And, clearly, the seeds come loose from the spike and explode into the air, when the dried spike is knocked about by 26 second graders!"

"Quite dramatic!" said Rachel.

"My students say the fluffy seeds look like "chicken fur."

"How are you going to clean that up?" asked Rachel.

Eve paused a moment then exclaimed, "I'm not sure we ever will!" Both teachers laughed as they enjoyed the special serendipity of exploding cattail spikes in the classroom.

༧༨

Jackson Hanson had been one of the second graders witnessing the show and tell in Mrs. Johnson's class. He thought the cattail fluff was "the coolest thing" although the soft piles of seeds reminded him of his own cats left behind at his old house. The golden white piles of seeds were just as soft as real cats' tails!

Jackson was, in fact, doing well as a new student at Lavonia Berber Elementary. His happy report to his family after just the first day of school was "I have lots of friends!" He also was pleased with Mrs. Johnson, his teacher. He told that "Mrs. Johnson goes fast!" Though she was challenging the class and stretching their capabilities, Jackson was proud of the progress he and his classmates were making with their studies.

Once when Julie came to pick Jackson up at the end of the school day, he announced, "Mrs. Johnson says she has high expectations of us."

"Oh? What does that mean, do you think?" responded Julie, glancing in the rearview mirror to see Jackson's face as he spoke.

"It means she thinks we are going to do lots of good stuff. She said we are the best group she's ever gotten to teach."

Julie's heart was lifted because she could tell that Jackson seemed ready to rise to his teacher's lofty aim for him and his fellow second graders.

On this show and tell day, Jackson was satisfied with his own presentation in front of the class, but he was concerned when his classmate Noah displayed a mangled, partly petrified animal body, saying it was a baby dinosaur! Jackson had been to a natural history museum, so he knew about fossils, but he couldn't figure how a classmate of his came up with a baby dinosaur! And though it was most certainly dead, and had a bit of an odor to prove it, the specimen wasn't a skeleton. Noah had everyone looking at the "teeth and claws and scales."

"It doesn't have wings yet," said Noah. "Maybe those grow when a dinosaur gets bigger."

As the period ended, Mrs. Johnson asked everyone to clean their hands since it was nearly lunch time, and they had all been touching "dinosaur scales." Jackson sidled up to Mrs. Johnson to say, "That wasn't really a dinosaur, was it?"

"Ah, most perceptive of you, Jackson! I will call you my zoologist of the day."

Jackson looked up at her face and could tell that she was being sincere in her compliment. He knew the words "perceptive" and "zoologist" because the class had added them to their word wall as those words had come up in their class discussions. "Why didn't you tell him that he was wrong?" asked Jackson. "I think that was an armadillo that had been run over by a car on the road."

Eve Johnson thought of the class expectations and asked Jackson, "What does our expectation say about 'every effort'?"

Jackson was able to answer because the class had memorized all 8 Expectations for Living. Those expectations formed the guide for how things operated in the class rather than there being a list of rules. He replied, "Expectation Number Six: We will recognize every effort and applaud it."

"Right," replied Mrs. Johnson. "Noah did a good job of telling facts about the animal body that he brought, even though he was wrong about the dinosaur identification. So we will applaud his effort for today, and then tomorrow we will correct the error and do some critical thinking to compare and contrast dinosaurs and armadillos. It is a good opportunity for us to learn. That's why we say mistakes are okay."

That made sense to Jackson, and he was primed to add to the discussion the next day. He could report to the class that nine-banded armadillos tend to jump straight in the air when surprised, so it was no wonder they are so often struck and killed by vehicles. "I guess I am like a zoologist," he thought with satisfaction.

∽∾

Jackson's brother Gabe had also had a good start to the school year, and he would credit the fact that almost everyone was thoughtful. He was happiest over the fact that he had already made new friends. He had tried to explain to his mom, "The kids are more social."

Julie wasn't sure what that meant or even if it was a good thing. "How are they more social?"

Gabe's response was "Well, they are just willing to start talking to me; not everyone, but many of them. Some of them have been classmates for a long time, but they make me feel like I belong, too, even though I am new."

Julie smiled to herself; she could imagine what a boost to self-esteem that sense of belonging provided for Gabe, and it was more like the camaraderie among classmates she had enjoyed during her own school experience.

Gabe had also been impressed by the principal, Mr. Wagner. He was always outside the front of the school building as the middle school crowd arrived; in fact, he was there every single day without regard for hot weather, freezing temperatures, strong winds, or even rain. Mr. Wagner kept an eye on things, but mainly he was out front so he could speak to all the student population as they entered the building to start the day. Gabe had also noticed more than once when he and his classmates returned to a classroom that had been vacant the preceding period, the white board was freshly cleaned, and there was a neatly lettered quotation written there. One that he remembered was, "Be glad when the job is difficult, not everyone can do it." One of the girls in his class told him that it was Mr. Wagner who slipped in and left the freshly cleaned boards with uplifting quotations.

Besides that, there was the Magic Triad!

"A magic what?" Lyle, Gabe's dad, had asked the first time he heard the phrase.

Gabe was only half listening to his dad, but after the question was repeated. Gabe said, "I don't know exactly, Dad. But you get the triad part. There are 3 things. A friendly word, a kind touch, and a smile. So when we go into the classroom, the teacher smiles, says something nice, and gives us a high five, maybe, or instead of the high five, the English teacher, Mrs. Wilson, gives us stickers."

Lyle's eyebrows shot up, and he said, "Stickers? Aren't you a little old for stickers?"

"Oh, it's okay. Mrs. Wilson found out that I play soccer, so she gives me soccer stickers. I think she bought them especially for me; she even had some major league soccer stickers."

"Really? That's impressive," said Lyle. "But how exactly is that magic?"

Gabe shrugged his shoulders, but then he said, "Well, it is like magic because it makes us all feel a little glad to be there."

Not every day had the Magic Triad quite done its job for Gabe. For instance, there was the day that he got hit in the mouth with Lowell's elbow. A set of the seventh graders were playing a serious game of hacky sack in the enclosed courtyard for a few minutes after lunch. As Gabe's classmate Lowell made a valiant effort to reach the small footbag before it hit the ground, he bashed Gabe right in the mouth with an elbow. It was an unintended injury, but it was made worse because of the braces on Gabe's teeth. Some of the inside of his lip was actually caught in the metal braces. Gabe's eyes were watering from the pain, and it took a bit to get his lip pulled loose from the pinch of metal braces. "Who knew you needed a mouthguard just to play hacky sack?" thought Gabe.

By the end of the school day, his lips were significantly swollen. He was ready to get home and get an ice pack for his injury.

Lowell caught him as he was collecting his books from his locker.

"Sorry about your mouth, man!" said Lowell.

"It's okay; I didn't think you did it on purpose." Gabe was trying to speak without moving his swollen lips. "I'm just surprised that I haven't gotten teased for my 'new look.' Not one person has said that it looks as if I've got a duck bill, and no one has called me 'camel lips.'"

"No mystery there!" said Lowell. "You know the expectation. 'We will not laugh at or make fun of a person's mistakes nor use sarcasm or putdowns.' So people aren't going to laugh at you. Besides that, if I were going to make any such comment, I wouldn't use duck bill or camel lips, I would call you a 'rosy-lipped batfish.' There is such a thing, you know."

"Nope," said Gabe. "I think you made it up!" The two headed out the door. Gabe was glad to be heading home to get ice for his swollen lip, but he was also glad that classmates hadn't laughed at his unfortunate appearance!

Gabe had pain of another kind a few days later. His lips were back to normal size, and the incident of the bashed braces was sinking into history. The boys' PE classes were playing dodge ball during gym since it was still too early for the coach to start basketball. At the end of the period, Coach Crowley blew his whistle. Activity in the gym held up except for a few balls that were still bouncing as the aftermath of whatever trajectory they were following when the whistle blew. "Balls in the rack!" announced the coach in his loud "gym voice."

On the far side of the gym, Gabe grabbed a ball and caught the eye of Lowell who was near the ball rack. Gabe pulled back and gave the ball a mighty heave in the direction of Lowell. He expected that Lowell would catch the ball and put it immediately into the ball rack as requested by the coach.

However, Zachary cut across the line of Gabe's throw, thinking to catch the ball himself and put it in the ball rack. The physics of the matter conspired to change that plan, because Zach hit the ball with his fingertips and sent it glancing off in an oblique angle that was totally opposite the direction of the ball rack.

Coach Crowley was unaware of the accurate description of what had just happened; he had only seen Gabe's throw out of the corner of his eye, followed by the ball flying wild after Zach's tap. To his mind, the instruction to put the balls away had been ignored. As soon as the balls were in the ball rack, he blew the whistle, gathered the class around him, and spoke with the intensity that teachers use when directions have been flaunted. "The young men on this squad are to follow directions." He looked right at Gabe and said, "I am sorely disappointed when team members do not follow direct requests." Gabe felt his face burning hot. Coach Crowley obviously had

Gabe pegged as a disrespectful, disobedient student. It gave Gabe a sick feeling.

When the group broke up to hit the lockers, Gabe went to the coach. He spoke respectfully, but he also made the case that he had been intending to follow the directions to put the balls away, and he had not meant to defy instructions. Coach Crowley listened, watched Gabe's face as he spoke, and then shook his hand and said, "Okay, Hanson, thanks for coming to speak to me, but I want you to know that I am counting on you to follow the coaching calls that I make."

Gabe had to hustle so that he could get changed out of gym clothes and make it to science class on time. The class topic of the day was plate tectonics. They were discussing the Kilauea volcano on the Big Island of Hawaii with some side comments about earthquakes since both geologic phenomena were related to the movement of the tectonic plates. Miss Sanford, the teacher, had an enthusiasm for the subject matter, and the class's interest was heightened by the Oreo cookies which they were using to illustrate the hard, rigid Earth's crust on top of a softer molten layer. Gabe and Lowell were certain that all visual aids should be edible! There was a knock at the door, but there was no observable response to the knock except from one of Gabe's classmates.

That one was Brianna; she quietly left her seat and went to the door. She was the class member who had the temporary assignment of answering the door, greeting visitors, taking messages, and, in all ways, attending to door traffic so that the teacher could continue teaching. Her role as a classroom concierge was designed not only to be an aid to the teacher but to give her experience at meeting people, making introductions, and serving the classroom family. Each of her classmates would also have a turn handling that responsibility and gaining poise in greeting visitors and making introductions.

"Coach Crowley, welcome to our classroom, how may I help you?" asked Brianna, breaking into a big smile when she recognized the coach.

Coach Crowley asked to speak to the class for just a moment. Brianna turned back to face Miss Sanford and waited quietly. Soon, Miss Sanford got to a point where discussion could be halted, she said, "Yes, Brianna?" That was Brianna's cue to introduce Coach Crowley and give him the floor.

Coach's message was brief. He just told the group that he had come to apologize to Gabe. He had misread Gabe's actions, and his reprimand of Gabe was unfounded. He went on to say, "I know I need to be a model of the behavior that we want from all of you students, and one of the things I need to model right now is to apologize when I've made a mistake. I misjudged your cooperation, Gabe. *'Right actions in the future are the best apologies for bad actions in the past,'* so I plan on doing better in the future about trusting your cooperative attitude, and I expect you to continue to earn that trust."

That was a day that Gabe would probably remember forever: Coach Crowley and his model of giving an apology when it was needed. A bad day for Gabe had just flipped to a really good day.

୨୦୧

Sarah was able to echo her siblings on the ease of making friends at school. She had found the other students at Center City High accepting and friendly. She had gotten to know a circle of classmates quickly and formed some friendships that were going to serve her well through the special time of being a senior. The self-pitying worry of where to sit in the cafeteria because she didn't know anyone was so quickly dropped that soon she didn't even remember it had been a concern.

She did note some differences that she would have called good changes from the way things were at her old school. For one thing, at the school where she had spent the previous years of her education, the classmates were fun and funny, but they mostly focused on just that: "being funny." Furthermore, there was much that she would describe as "goofing off" "goofing around," and generally just being "goofballs." She counted them as great friends, but she could see now that they were wasting most of their time. At Center City, the students, though friendly, also seemed bent on achieving excellence, and without fail, the teachers had all posted quotations that kept everyone's mind on excellence. She copied some of them in her notebooks as she went to classes:

"The rung of a ladder was never meant to rest upon, but only to hold a man's foot long enough to enable him to put the other somewhat higher." – Thomas Huxley

"Don't bother just to be better than your contemporaries or predecessors. Try to be better than yourself." – William Faulkner

"The man on top of the mountain didn't fall there." – Vince Lombardi

Sarah observed a difference not only in students at the new school, but she also believed the teachers really knew their subject matter. She told her parents, "I've learned more in the first few weeks of school than I learned in all of last year. I was surprised at what I did not know." She was impressed that the teachers engaged directly with students for the full class periods. The teachers' commitment of time and effort to the classes made Sarah believe the classes must also be worth her time. She appreciated that the teachers were looking out for the students as people and as young adults whose character development mattered. Test scores were important for the school, but the quest for those high marks was not so paramount that it squelched the nurturing of qualities vital in day-to-day living.

Sarah especially enjoyed Mrs. Baker, the teacher for the Government and Politics class. Mrs. Baker talked to the class about passion and focus for what they wanted to do with their lives. Besides the class content, she helped the students review how to study, how to problem-solve, how to engage in conversation, and how to look at both new and old ideas.

One of the highlights for Sarah during the first two weeks of school had been the creed-writing committee. When senior class officers were chosen, Sarah was not nominated for any position, but she was not surprised since she was new. However, the class subsequently voted to write their own creed for the climax of their high school careers. The school had a creed which the class had memorized and recited since their freshman year, but now they wanted their very own creed, one which they developed themselves. The idea had been planted by their class advisor, Mrs. Baker, who used her government and political science background to foster the idea that the creed would be more meaningful to them if they crafted the wording themselves.

The creed-writing cohort was to be composed of the class officers and then each officer could choose an additional senior to be on the committee. Melissa, the class reporter, snagged Sarah to be a part of the group. Mrs. Baker started them off: they reviewed the Great Expectations Life Principles, wrote essays on what they thought was most important in life, and studied examples of creeds including those from the U.S. military; then they formed groups and wrote statements containing the values that fit their class.

Mrs. Baker told the group, "Begin with a statement that says who you are and then a sentence that describes you." Additionally, she gave the example of the Army and Army National Guard Creed:

> I am an American Soldier.
> I am a Warrior and a member of a team.
> I serve the people of the United States
> and live the Army Values.

Next, the committee groups had put together their statements and decided which sentences should be eliminated, reworded, or combined. Finally, they settled on the order of their statements. Mrs. Baker said they must come to a consensus. This was not a time for majority rule. They had to all agree or rework things until that unanimous agreement could be reached.

It was a more involved process than Sarah had imagined, but then she realized as they finished and all agreed on the final product that it was truly meaningful to her and the committee. She hoped it would ring true for all the rest of the class as well.

They began the creed with the line "We are the seniors of Center City High School," and then they followed through the whole creed with the plural wording rather than using the singular pronoun, "I." Tyler, the class president, a lively, funny student leader who earned everyone's affection, put forth the second line of the creed to be "We are loved, and we appreciate our families and teachers." Some of the committee had objected, saying that it was rather vain to claim that they were loved, but Tyler insisted that it was a true statement, and, finally, the group relented. Sarah was glad that they had done so, because as the class began to use the creed and recite it on different occasions, she watched her classmates stand taller and smile bigger each time they declared "We are loved!" They said the words, and they came true.

As the committee wrapped up the creed-writing process, Melissa was ready in her role as class reporter. She suggested that they have a creed-signing ceremony, invite the superintendent to come, and allow her as reporter to get the local newspaper to print a picture and her article on the whole process. The boys all voted in agreement with her motion after they had amended it to include some food as part of the ceremony.

After the creed signing, which fit nicely in one of the class meeting slots on the school calendar, Melissa's article was printed in the community newspaper. Sarah spoke to Mrs. Baker and said, "Thanks for letting me be a part of the creed writing."

"Oh, you are so welcome, Sarah. Your group did an excellent job. Not all classes write a class creed, you know. Some do personal creeds."

"Hmmm. I could see that would be good, but since I was on the committee, I feel like this is my creed. I like that it belongs to all of us as a class."

Mrs. Baker was delighted. She was particularly impressed with the line that the students had included which said, "We will utilize every day given to us to the fullest, realizing we will never have another shot at today, right here, right now." She knew that to be a true sentiment even more than the students did. Their year would fly by.

"Good bye, Mrs. Baker," said Sarah. Then she quoted the last line of the creed as her parting comment, "We seize the day!"

"*Carpe diem!*" replied Mrs. Baker. Then she added, "Now put your creed into deed."

༄

As the first full month of school quickly closed out with all its assignments, events, and activities, Lyle gave his folks a call to report on the family and how things were going in their new home. His dad was interested to hear the full account of the new house, Lyle's work, and Julie's satisfaction with her shopping sources in Center City. Then his dad asked, "How are the kids?"

"They are all three pretty happy," replied Lyle. "They were worried about making friends, but their interaction with other kids has been especially good. They seemed surprised at the start that other students would talk to them. They thought a new school would be a bitter pill to take, but the school days are sweetened by the general culture of the school."

"Another thing is the fact that the schools – all the school sites: elementary, middle school, and high school – promote what they call life principles. The kids talk about them sometimes; Jackson was even explaining to me one day what *esprit de corps* is. At work, I've been pushing our company's "commitment to quality" with the team that I oversee, and then when I was driving home last Friday, there on a huge roadside sign sponsored by a city organization was a billboard promotion of "commitment," the school's life principle of the week! The students, and now even the town, are all on the same page. It is pretty powerful."

Sarah had come into the kitchen while Lyle finished his phone conversation with her granddad. Lyle was aware she had come in, but he didn't pay attention to the fact that she was shuffling through the pages in one of her notebooks. When he said his goodbyes, Sarah said, "Hi, Dad. How's Papa Bill?"

"I told him we would plan to drive to see them at Thanksgiving." Then looking at the paper that Sarah had pulled out of her notebook and handed him, he asked, "What's this?"

Sarah smiled smugly. "It is a quotation that we used at school last week. We don't know for sure, but it may be words from Abraham Lincoln. You can use it with your workers when you talk about commitment." She restacked her books, grabbed a banana, and headed up to her room, leaving Lyle to read the words on commitment.

"Commitment is what transforms a promise into reality. It is the words that speak boldly of your intentions. And the actions which speak louder than the words. It is making the time when there is none. Coming through time after time after time, year after year after year. Commitment is the stuff character is made of; the power to change the face of things. It is the daily triumph of integrity over skepticism."

ABRAHAM LINCOLN

Chapter 3

In the Spotlight, Not on the Spot

*"And the days dwindle down
To a precious few,
September, November –
And these few precious days,
I'll spend with you,
These golden days, I'll spend with you."*
MAXWELL ANDERSON

November brought holiday bustle, fewer hours of daylight, and an invitation for parents to come to "Rise and Shine," which was Lavonia Berber Elementary School's daily morning assembly. Julie loaded parcels to mail which contained the diverse items she had recently sold on the Internet: a 1955 comic book, a file of black and white photos of movie scenes which had been left behind in an old theatre, and an elegant Italian art glass Christmas tree figurine. She could stop at the post office and still be at school in time for the assembly. She did not want to be late because the daily student meetings did not last long.

Arriving at the school just in time, Julie hurried to the door of the elementary building. On the way, she glanced at the lettering painted all along the overhead cove of the entrance portico: ATTITUDE, CHARACTER, CHARITY, COMMON SENSE, COMPASSION, COOPERATION… Julie didn't stop to read all the life principles, but she knew that the students were learning, not only to define the words, but also to assimilate those qualities into their conduct. Just the week before, she had received a pleasing email from Eve Johnson, Jackson's teacher. The class had studied the life principle of Honesty, and Mrs. Johnson's message said that Jackson had demonstrated commendable honesty in class. Just as Mrs. Johnson had begun to dictate a spelling test, Jackson's hand shot up. When he was called upon, he stood and said, "Mrs. Johnson, the spelling list is still posted by the marker board. We would all be able to copy the words." Julie and Lyle were proud of Jackson's conscientiousness; they welcomed the school's attention to a culture that builds good citizenship.

They were also gratified that Jackson had mastered the spelling words so that the opportunity to copy answers was not a temptation to him. He and his classmates had reviewed their words in a technique that turned into original works of art which were now posted in the hallway. Julie saw the display on her way to the gym where the students were gathering for the morning assembly. Jackson had told about the project; he called it "scribble spelling." Students had drawn big scribbles on their individual pages with large spaces within their scribbles. Then using colored pencils, they had written their spelling words repeatedly to fill the spaces within their scribbles. There were post-it note feedback comments on each paper from Mrs. Johnson. Julie had already noticed from earlier trips to school that the teachers consistently gave students oral or written feedback on their work. For the spelling scribbles, Mrs. Johnson praised the originality that the assignment had inspired, pointed out color combinations the class had studied in art class, and noted the shapes that appeared within the squiggles. Julie could see that it was an interesting way to practice spelling words and integrate some elements of art, and she knew that Jackson liked the fact that Mrs. Johnson had many ways to display the work that he and his classmates did.

Julie followed several other parents into the gym and joined them in standing along the wall where they could watch but not be in the way. Most of the students were already packed in orderly rows with their classmates in the open space of the all-purpose room. They were intently watching and following the movements of Principal Aransus directing the group in stretches and steps and bends and "moves" while a recording of "We Are the World" played in the background. Julie recognized some of the movements from one of her aerobics classes, but she did not realize that Principal Aransus was intent on gaining the benefits of movement for her students based on her studies of brain research. Julie could just see that the students were having fun. As the music ended, a third grade student, who had been on the stage during the warm-up, stepped to the microphone; he called out "Shining stars are who we are!"

Then the student body called back, "Shining stars go far, far, far!" This served as the opening to the Rise and Shine Assembly that was meant everyday to be a call to excellence and to remind teachers and students that they were being held to high expectations.

Other third graders took turns leading different portions of the assembly. Julie thought it was impressive that they had the poise to speak loudly and clearly before such a large group. Students remained standing for the flag salute while a picture of a soldier, the son of one of the teachers, was projected onto the screen at the front of the room. The music teacher led everyone in singing "You're a Grand Old Flag." Julie was fascinated by the exuberance of the singing and the fact that even the littlest children knew the words to the flag salute. The third grade emcee led the assembly in reciting the school creed and then a cheer for the cute first grade twin girls who were celebrating their birthday that day.

Next, Rachel Mullins's first graders took the stage to present their lexicon. Their word of the day was *dependability*, which was also the life principle for the week. They displayed a chart with the syllables of the word written on lines drawn like stair steps, and the label *NOUN* to identify the word's part of speech. These were aspects of the word identification skills they studied in class. Nicholas, Mrs. Mullins's talker, had volunteered to announce the definition of the word and give a sentence example. Then he said, "Hickety-Pickety Bumble Bee, can you say this word with me?"

The students all knew the routine and chanted "de-pend-a-bil-i-ty!"

"Let's all clap it," exclaimed Nicholas, and with answering enthusiasm, the students called out the syllables of the word and clapped for each one.

"Let's all snap it!" he said.

After finger snapping for the syllables, Nicholas led the group in chanting, "Clap, snap, de-pend-a-bil-i- ty!"

Rachel had read the Dr. Seuss book *Horton Hatches the Egg* to the class. The book tells the story of Horton the elephant, who is tricked into sitting on a bird's egg while the irresponsible mother bird leaves. Horton endures many hardships but remains dependable and on the job. Nicholas concluded the lesson on the life principle of dependability with words from that story: "I said what I meant, and I meant what I said, an elephant's faithful one hundred percent." Then together the first grade class members shouted spiritedly, "Be dependable!"

The program was concluded by Mrs. Cochran, the school counselor, who stepped before the assembly with an announcement. "Accolades to five classes who averaged ninety-five percent or higher on their math challenges this week," she said. In an on-going effort to help raise test scores, Mrs. Cochran studied the test data from the various standardized tests and tailor-made short review assignments for each class, specific to their deficient areas. Her review pages were a supplement to the more detailed efforts by the teachers who use test data for individual students to target content to be re-taught. The weekly Cochran Challenge stirred up some competition that motivated extra student effort and some student-to-student teaching. Then, students and teachers joined one another in celebrating the successes. On this day when Julie was at Rise and Shine, Mrs. Cochran was operating with a Serengeti theme. She was wearing a safari coat and a pith helmet, and she presented a small toy giraffe to the class with the highest average score on their mastery pages. "Be like the giraffe and keep on stretching higher!" she said.

At the last celebration for the math challenge champions, the students began to move out of the gym. With calming classical music by Mozart on the sound system, the students followed an orderly pattern and moved quickly and quietly as they exited the gym. Julie stepped to intercept Mrs. Johnson. "I am Jackson's mom, Julie Hanson," she said. "I want to thank you for all the ways you are helping Jackson and his classmates."

Mrs. Johnson beamed. She appreciated having her efforts acknowledged as much as the children did. "Thank you so much, Mrs. Hanson! Jackson is a treasure! I'm so glad to have him in class this year."

Julie left feeling quite impressed with Lavonia Berber Elementary; however, she had departed the school premises before Mrs. Aransus had problematic third graders Dalton and Wesley reporting to her office. Rarely would a Lavonia Berber student be brought to the principal from recess or a class for fighting, but these two boys had not yet arrived at a consistently amicable relationship with one another even though the school year was well underway. Mrs. Aransus had a set procedure for student arguments; it was part of the discipline with dignity and logic that she and the teachers employed. Each child could tell her what happened, but each was only allowed to begin his sentence with "I..." They each had 60 seconds to talk. After that, she always asked: "Now what? What can you do to prevent this from happening again?" Often there was silence, but occasionally the offenders would actually offer good suggestions. To end the situation, they would shake hands, look each other in the eye and say "Let's be friends."

"I'm sorry" was a phrase Mrs. Aransus and the Lavonia Berber teachers asked that the students not use because it was too easy just to say those words and make no change. Instead they offered the students a choice from phrases such as "I apologize for..." or "May I try again to..."

The principal and the teachers had all explained and practiced these procedures for handling student discord. If a situation with conflict between students persisted, then Mrs. Aransus or the teacher working with the children would help the students role-play how to handle the problem. The role-playing would only take five minutes or so.

On this day, Dalton and Wesley were presented to Mrs. Aransus by a teacher for fighting at recess, yet again. She reminded them of the procedure; they looked at each other and said, "Mrs. Aransus, can we just shake hands and promise to do better from now on?" The principal promptly gave each of them a hug and praised them for solving their own problem, and said "I am counting on you as *dependable* young men who will keep your word." She knew it was possible there could be a repeat episode of a disagreement between the two, but now she had the option of reminding them of the promise they had just made.

༄༅

When November 11th came up on the calendar, it was Lyle's turn to go to a school assembly; Gabe had given him a special invitation to come. The assembly was the middle school's Veterans Day Program, and Gabe was excited! Miss Sanford had helped his class prepare a mime presentation to accompany a recording of the song "I'm Proud to Be an American." The pantomime matched Gabe's joy at being on the move; this was with music which made it even better, and he was able to mimic all the movements that Miss Sanford had shown the group to go with the lyrics of the song. Miss Sanford helped the students round up army camo clothing, but Gabe felt as if his camouflage cargo pants were especially good. His super-shopper mom had purchased them for him. Besides all that, they got to wear mime makeup on their faces! Jacob, the tallest seventh grade boy, carried the flag on stage, and the class's posture showed the strictest formality and respect for the flag. Beyond the excitement of performing, the presentation was meaningful to the class because Miss Sanford had integrated information about military history in their science class. In fact, they had been astonished by the connections between military history and some scientific studies and developments. The swing into history as part of a science class wasn't a surprise to those who knew Miss Sanford. She consistently blended other subject matter into the lessons she taught and related class content to the real world. She even took groups of students to Space Camp and also to Sea Camp during the summers. The sign outside her classroom door set the high expectations for what students would experience under her tutelage:

WELCOME TO ROOM 8! Here's what you can expect: Learning from mistakes, respect for all, hard work, laughter, teamwork, and, did I mention, hard work? In Room 8, we dream big because we believe in ourselves. We talk to important people because we are important. We hold classroom meetings because every voice is needed. We investigate because we are professionals. We learn life skills because we are productive citizens. We enjoy and appreciate every moment because life is precious. We learn the importance of becoming lifelong learners. Get ready to have the time of your life in Room 8! *It will be an experience you will never forget!*

As the mime presentation concluded with the words "We won't forget the men who died" still ringing in everyone's ears, Lyle, along with the whole audience, was touched by the poignant reminder of the serious realities behind Veterans Day.

Miss Sanford was happy that the students had taken the patriotic project to heart, but she was particularly pleased with the participation of Riley. He was a seventh grader and new to the school like Gabe, but, unlike Gabe, he had not made friends. He chose most of the time to stay as close to the fringe of whatever activity was going on as possible, and he never raised his hand to answer a question in class. Sometimes he even stayed outside in the cold courtyard until the last minute before class commenced. Since Riley was new to the school and his records were not complete, it had taken Miss Sanford and the other teachers a full nine weeks of school before they learned that he did not hear well. But with special attention and extra practice and a strategic placement near one of the sound system speakers, Riley had done the mime presentation with precision and passion. Later in the day, Mr. Wagner, the principal, slipped by Room 8 to congratulate the mime troupe, and he made a particular effort to compliment Riley. Miss Sanford was gratified that the environment in the school and in her classroom was non-threatening so that the group of seventh graders, including Riley, was willing to take the risk of performing before the whole school.

Other classes for Gabe and his classmates also integrated lessons that related to the real world. The history classes taught by Mr. Nelson were notably engaging for the seventh graders. As a retired military man, Mr. Nelson retained his loud voice, straight posture, flawless grooming and dress, commitment to orderliness, and insistence on devotion to duty. Every inch of his classroom walls was covered with flags, maps, pictures of Presidents, newspaper clippings, and historical documents. He often set up his classroom to resemble the floor of the U.S. House of Representatives. He acted as the presiding official at the front of the room, and individual students were called to stand in the space at the front and center called the "well." He asked review questions, and the student standing at a podium in the well answered, addressing the class, and speaking in complete sentences. The students who were seated in a semi-circle around the well had their notes and books as references. If the student in the well could not answer, then he or she had the prerogative to request that the question be answered by a classmate. "Mr. Nelson, may I call on my esteemed colleague Gabriel Hanson to answer that question?" Students got practice speaking before the whole class, and the group had effective reviews prior to upcoming tests. The learners were put "in the spotlight," but not "on the spot" because they could always call on someone else to handle a question they couldn't answer, and students who were at their desks could look up answers they didn't remember.

Gabe and his classmates also came to appreciate the challenge that Mr. Nelson had given them of keeping the section of the hall that housed their seventh grade lockers looking as if it were ready to pass military barracks inspection. The hall cleanup crew rotated through the week. Mr. Nelson had a timer set to ring five minute before the end of the school day; when the timer rang, whichever two-person student crew was assigned for the day stepped out to the hallway and made a last sweep to check for any misplaced paper or other fallen trash. If it was a day when dirt or leaves had been tracked in, the crew got a broom and dustpan and swept the hallway clean. By this time of the school year, there was usually very little to do during clean up, because the students had adopted the habit of orderliness and took pride in keeping their section of the hallway clean. They claimed boasting rights for maintaining the cleanest hallway in the building, and Mr. Nelson was pleased to see ways that the students were assuming responsibilities.

"Rise to the challenges that life presents you. You can't develop genuine character and ability by sidestepping adversity and struggle."
VIKAS RUNWAL

Chapter 4

Giving, and Giving Thanks

"No one is useless in the world who lightens the burdens of another."
CHARLES DICKENS

In mid-November, Principal Aransus arranged for substitute elementary teachers so Rachel Mullins and five of her colleagues from Lavonia Berber were able to be gone from school for the day to attend the Great Expectations Fall Conference. Rachel was muddling through her preparations for being gone from her classroom. "How is a person supposed to get all the necessary information written down for a substitute teacher?" she lamented to her neighbor teacher, Eve Johnson.

Eve stepped back into her own classroom and returned in a moment with a "Classroom Handbook." It was a guide she had formulated for any occasion when she needed to be gone from her class. The notebook had quotations, class schedules, and test procedures. It also contained the class motto, class creed, and a description of all classroom procedures. "When I leave the handbook for a substitute, I slip in a page with a note asking the substitute teacher to write down all the good things that happen during the time I am gone, and the things that need improvement. It is one way I can model organization and responsibility for my students."

Rachel liked the idea and hurried to compile her own classroom handbook, at least a first edition of one. She could also see the benefit of having such a handbook to show parents at parent-teacher conferences, and the handbook preparation helped Rachel feel at ease about being gone from her students for a day.

At the Great Expectations Fall Conference, there were breakout discussions on a number of different topics. Rachel wished to attend several of the sessions that were offered, but she finally chose one called "Classroom Management," led by an impressive teacher who, Rachel later learned, serves as an instructor at Great Expectations Summer Institute sessions during June and July. The focus of the class was on the GE tools for effective classroom management with emphasis on the "7 Keys of the GE Discipline Philosophy." It fit Rachel's needs beautifully, and she enjoyed visiting with the other teachers in the session. She left the conference with refreshed enthusiasm for her work as a teacher and some practical strategies to put to use in her own classroom.

ೞ⋞

Soon after the day when Rachel and the other Center City teachers had returned from GE Fall Conference, everyone's mind turned to the upcoming Thanksgiving break. The weather made a shift to bone-chilling cold, but teachers and students alike were glad for the holiday interruption to the hectic obligations of school. At the Hansons' house, Julie was doing holiday baking and directing everyone in getting their bags packed. The family would pile in the car in the morning to drive the 295 miles to Papa Bill and Gram's house for the official turkey dinner on Thursday. In the midst of the hubbub, Julie had opened up her computer on the kitchen counter where she was finishing pecan pies to see if the antique license plate that she had up in an online auction had sold. It was a 1910 dealer's car tag labeled "Wichita, Kansas." The porcelain on steel tag which had only three numbers must have been one of the very first Kansas car tags. When she checked the final sale price, she uttered a shocked exclamation.

"What's the matter, Mom?" asked Sarah.

"The license plate that I bought at a garage sale last summer for a dollar just sold for $1,800!"

This was especially good news because sales had been slow for Julie's merchandise through the summer, and then she had not even tried to sell anything while the family was in the midst of their move. This income was welcome.

"Wow, Mom! That's great!" said Sarah. "Gabe! Jackson!" she called. "We need to give Mom a celebration; she just sold an antique car tag for $1,800!"

Gabe and Jackson came tumbling into the kitchen. "A Standing *O*!" said Gabe. That was his favorite of the various celebrations that he and his classmates gave one another to recognize successes.

Immediately the three children stood at attention, raised their arms to form circles above their heads, and intoned, "Ohhhhhhhhhhhhhhhhhh!"

Lyle had just arrived home and stepped into the house from the garage in time to witness the impromptu celebration that was going on. "What are you doing?" he asked.

"It's a celebration!" said Jackson.

Sarah added, "It's a Standing *O*. Like a standing ovation, but we just stand and say 'Ohhhh.'"

Lyle was still puzzled, "Because…?"

Julie got to tell the news, "I just sold that 1910 license plate for $1,800!"

"Oh, my! $1,800!" exclaimed Lyle. Then he straightened up, threw his arms up in an O, and mimicked the children's "Ohhhhhhhhhh!"

It was a happy family moment with a celebration of the financial windfall, but also sweet were the laughter that followed and the anticipation of a holiday ahead.

By the next day, the family was all loaded into the van and on the road to the grandparents. Even though frigid weather had settled in, the Hansons' road trip was smooth. By the halfway mark, they stopped for lunch and a restroom break. Lyle and the boys were waiting for the ladies when they heard a cry of dismay coming from inside the restroom. That first exclamation from Sarah was followed by a couple more shrieks and the familiar wail of "Mo-o-o-m!" that meant Sarah needed help from her mother.

In a few moments, Sarah and her mom emerged, and Gabe said, "What was all the squawking about?"

The family had pulled into a newly remodeled truck stop on their route. The sinks in the restroom were fitted with automatic water and soap dispensers. Those fixtures had the newest "touchless" feature which made them fully automatic so they pour out water or soap as the user merely waves a hand. However, in trying to get the water "on" in the sink, Sarah had set her handbag on the counter. The placement of the bag triggered the outpouring of soap onto the bag; Sarah pulled the bag away, and her hand movement caused more soap to spew out. Her subsequent efforts had just led to soap and more soap on the counter.

Just before Thanksgiving break, Mrs. Baker's Government and Politics class had been giving speeches on the topic of "Personal Responsibility." Sarah had been especially impressed with Sam Goodwin's speech. His effectiveness, at least for Sarah, was aided by his polite manners, great smile, and blue eyes. Yes, she had noticed his eyes. He had quoted a list that he called "Rules of the House." It included common sense guidelines, such as: "If you open it, close it." "If you turn it on, turn it off." "If you borrow it, return it." and so on.

Since Sarah had truly focused on Sam – and consequently his speech – she now felt compelled to follow "Rule Number 8" for which he had said, "If you make a mess, clean it up." She had certainly made a soap mess, but now, every stroke she made to wipe up the soap caused more foamy suds to shoot out onto the counter. The restroom was equipped with a high velocity hand dryer which promised to dry one's hands in fifteen seconds, but which provided no paper towels for cleaning up a mess! Fortunately, Julie had a pack of tissues in her bag, and she was able, with a talent that belongs perhaps uniquely to moms, to make a couple of swipes to wipe up the sudsy soap quickly enough that the automatic dispenser couldn't react.

After Julie explained what had happened, and Sarah elaborated on Sam Goodwin and "If you make a mess, clean it up," the brothers spent a good part of the remaining trip making up additional "rules."

"If you find the cookie tub, you can eat the cookies." "If you have the TV remote in your hand, you get to pick the programs and change the channel every fifteen seconds if you want." "If your socks stink, you can't sit on the sofa." "If you say, 'Hey, guys, watch this,' you are going to get in trouble for what follows." "If I like it, it is mine." "If it is broken, it is yours."

Lyle finally said, "If the Dad says, 'Enough,' then the rule-making game ends!"

೧೦

The holiday at Papa Bill and Gram's house was great; the family had an entertaining visit and consumed a good part of the traditional Thanksgiving food that Gram had prepared. The grandparents were particularly impressed with Jackson's poise and communication skills since he was only a second grader. He and his classmates had been practicing how to meet a new person by shaking hands, looking him in the eye, making introductions, and then conversing. So when Jackson went with Papa Bill to the community center to drop off some gift donations, he was well prepared to meet and greet some of his grandfather's friends.

"You did a good job introducing yourself and striking up a conversation with Mr. Davis and Mrs. Barnes. Where did you learn to do that?" asked Papa Bill.

Jackson didn't realize it was particularly impressive, "Oh, we usually greet people who visit our classroom; I got to introduce the superintendent one time. We have a special chair where visitors can sit and a sign outside the door of our classroom that asks visitors to 'please knock.' Mrs. Johnson says that we are helpers for her when we take care of guests."

Papa Bill looked forward to his next opportunity to visit with his community center friends because he was counting on collecting their compliments on his talented grandboy.

༄༅

On the day after Thanksgiving, the family hit the road for their return trip. "Aren't we going to go to Black Friday sales?" asked Gabe.

"No, not today," said Julie.

"Are you sure you don't want to go shopping?" persisted Gabe.

"Why? What do you want to buy?" asked Lyle.

"Well, I wasn't going to buy anything, but in math class we spent two days last week learning how to calculate our money savings if we buy something that is some per cent off in price. Just tell me the price and the per cent, and I'll figure it out! AND I can also calculate how much you have to pay in taxes."

"That's useful," said Julie.

"Mr. Van Arkel said it was something related to the real world, and that we would need it for Black Friday sales," said Gabe.

"Hold on to that skill; we will be going shopping soon," replied Julie. She was impressed, because she couldn't remember that she paid attention to such information when she was a seventh grader.

◈

In no time, the Thanksgiving vacation from school was over. The Hanson kids didn't mind going back to school, even though the holiday had been sweet, because now there were only three weeks to go before Christmas break. But when the family returned home, there was bad news on the local scene. On the coldest night right before Thanksgiving, there had been a raging fire in an apartment building in town. There was no sprinkler system in the building because it had been built before they were required, and the fire spread quickly. The newspaper told that the building was totally engulfed in flames by the time the fire department arrived, and six families lost their homes and all of their belongings. It wasn't until school was back in session that Gabe learned Jacob, his tall classmate who had waved the flag in the mime presentation of "I'm Proud to Be an American," was one of the victims of the fire. He and his family had survived the fire, but his dad was injured when he had jumped from the second floor balcony to escape the flames, and their possessions were destroyed. It made the Hansons pause to consider their own blessings of safety and comfort, and to think about how they might extend help to those who had suffered such loss.

Riley Granrud, Gabe's seventh grade classmate who had been so reticent because of his hearing impairment, had grown remarkably in self-assurance since his role in the mime troupe on Veterans Day. He was the one to approach Miss Sanford about the class's donating some household essentials to classmate Jacob and his family because of their losses in the apartment fire. Miss Sanford readily accepted the idea and helped Riley direct the class on details of the effort. She congratulated the group on putting the life principle of compassion into action. Beyond that highlight, she was so delighted that it was Riley who now was taking the leadership role in helping his classmate's family because she remembered Riley in September when he wouldn't even speak to others at school. When she offered special recognition to Riley, he said, "It is just Expectation Number 5; 'We will help one another whenever possible.'" In spite of Riley's dismissal of his role in making a difference, Miss Sanford celebrated in her own mind because she could tell Riley's self-esteem had been lifted, and his leadership on the project was a beautiful way for him to experience success.

※

With classes back underway, Sarah was considering the option of signing up for the drama production next semester. She had never done any acting or anything like it, but she was impressed by the drama coach, Mrs. Barton. She was a petite, energetic woman who always seemed to be smiling. She called Sarah by name even though Sarah was not in any of her classes. Mrs. Barton regularly wore school colors on ball game days and won teacher costume competitions since she could select from a whole drama wardrobe for homecoming dress-up days. Sarah remembered one day when Mrs. Barton was lugging a big bongo drum through the hall, and she had seen her on the topmost part of a tall ladder, rigging stage lights.

Sarah read over the handout that Mrs. Barton had set out for students who planned to participate in the spring drama production. The announcement told that the presentation would be in the style of 16th century Italian Commedia Dell'Arte, a form of theatre featuring masked character "types." It all sounded quite impressive, and Sarah could imagine telling family and friends, "Oh, yes, I'll be in the Commedia Dell'Arte presentation this spring!"

Sarah did read Mrs. Barton's paragraph telling how participation in drama could build all the effective communication skills that students would need in the future as well as instill some high standards for fulfilling one's personal responsibilities, but she didn't pay a great deal of attention to that information. She calculated that she would just get a back stage job and have fun without the stress of memorizing lines or standing before an audience.

Sarah mentioned the idea of being a part of the drama production to her folks as the family drove to the high school gym for a basketball game. She was surprised by how enthusiastic her mom was. "That will be great!" said Julie. Julie didn't elaborate on the fact that she had played Annie Oakley in a show when she was in high school. The whole experience had been memorable, and now as she thought back, being in drama was one of her favorite high school memories.

As the Hansons made their way into the gym with its smells of popcorn and sounds of the pep band playing, they moved along a corridor that circled the gym at the level just above the highest bleacher seats. The hallway had been turned into an exhibit area by the humanities class. "Oh, look!" said Jackson. His attention was caught because the displays, prepared by the sophomore students, featured interesting scale model museums. Class members had used art museum catalogs to collect pictures of works of art. Then they each created multiple rooms in a scale model museum by means of various configurations of cardboard boxes. Next, each student curator mounted pictures of the artwork which he had selected and added labels that described the art including dimensions, the medium used, and the artist. The project not only helped students learn about the pieces of art they had chosen, but it also integrated math as they calculated the scale of their museum walls to match the scale of at least one of their pieces of art. They had free rein to decorate their buildings. Some students used doorway molding, floor carpets, and others pictured details that they trimmed from old copies of *Architectural Design* magazines. Other students with a talent for art design drew in their own details and added paint.

"Look at this one," said Gabe. It was a model museum put together by a student who had his thoughts on all the practicalities. The student designer had drawn in exit signs, fire extinguishers, postings about "no smoking," and even arrows for the museum restrooms! The multi-faceted assignment had also integrated the use of computer capability for graphic design as students prepared trifold brochures for their "museums."

The humanities students also had the opportunity to practice some public speaking because each student/curator acted as the docent for his or her museum. The class members had taken turns giving classmates the tour of the museum exhibits. The exhibits were clearly kid-made, but ball game patrons who walked past could tell that the students had been immersed in art work for the preparation of their projects, and some students, like Gabe and Jackson, were intrigued by the possibilities of making scale models themselves.

໒ຂ

Sarah wasn't making scale models or doing the same project as the humanities students, but there were many varied assignments. She was to do some memory work, recitation, or writing everyday; and the pace had picked up in her math class. Her math teacher, Mr. Dobbs, was a retired engineer, and he loved math. Before he attended Great Expectations training, he did not make very good connections with his students. It seemed to him that the pupils should be just as excited as he was about doing math problems. In many ways he seemed like an absent-minded professor because he was so engrossed in mathematics that sometimes he seemed oblivious to other matters. But after he attended GE training, he began to make some good associations with his students. Sarah liked how careful and precise he was in making the expectations for his classes clear, and she noticed that he had a bulletin board in his room that was always filled with newspaper clippings featuring news about the Center City high school students – band competitions, livestock shows, sports events, rodeos, and speech contests. There was even an article about the school's first participation in a robotics competition. He was able to relate the math that he was teaching to the math he had used in his engineering career as he had traveled to many faraway places in the world, and he gave students "risk pads" and asked them to come up with solutions to problems that he posed rather than having them wait passively for him to provide "the right answer." Mr. Dobbs and other teachers at the high school really sought student understanding of concepts. They identified students' weak areas and then gave them the additional time they needed to master core concepts and elevate their learning to the next level.

The other thing Sarah had become accustomed to in Mr. Dobbs class was his question-answer procedure. When he posed a question, the responding student was to repeat the whole question orally and then give the answer in a complete sentence, rather than merely giving a quick one or two word answer. Hearing the entire question and then an answer which clearly explained what information was being relayed really helped her understand the concept under discussion.

As the last weeks of the semester approached, Sarah and her classmates found a sign reading "The Scriptorium" above the door to the English classroom. The label hung there for a series of days when the seniors were writing. It was an interesting touch that their classroom had been labeled with the term that meant literally "a place for writing." It was originally a term used to refer to a room in medieval European monasteries devoted to writing, copying, and illuminating of manuscripts by monastic scribes. Sarah and her classmates were not dealing with someone else's manuscripts, rather with their own writing, but the term tied back to some of the interesting facts that they had studied earlier about Geoffrey Chaucer in English literature. It seemed to Sarah that it helped to make sense of things when material was reviewed and then connected to upcoming lessons. It caught the class's imagination when they learned that the remains of Rosslyn Castle in Scotland which was featured in the novel and movie *The Da Vinci Code* contained a scriptorium!

The other thing going on in the English classroom was the push for enriched vocabulary. The senior English teacher, Mrs. Trotter, had hung up a shower curtain, a rather simple shower curtain, but it was printed with a hundred of the vocabulary words that appear on the SAT test. The seniors were challenged, not only to learn the words, but to use them as they answered oral discussion questions in class. If one of the seniors correctly used the secret word of the day which Mrs. Trotter had selected from the list on the shower curtain, she would launch a class celebration. Mrs. Trotter's students elevated their overall vocabulary usage in their efforts to be the one to use the secret SAT vocabulary word of the day.

Mrs. Trotter also displayed a big wall chart of Greek and Latin root words. It was always on hand for students to reference, and they quickly learned that knowing root words, prefixes, and suffixes expanded their vocabulary comprehension almost automatically. For example, it made sense to them that since the root word *aud* has to do with "hearing" and "listening," then that fit with *audio*, a word they already knew, and they could surmise that *audiology*, which was a new word to them, is a study of hearing. The Greek and Latin root words chart was almost like a silent teaching partner, helping the students expand their verbal capabilities without taking direct class instruction time.

Then there was Sarah's science class. Mr. Swindall frequently gave the group hands-on activities that clarified concepts to be learned. One day he came in with little round markers appropriated from a children's board game and some foam beverage coasters. The class was divided into teams, and they had guidelines for how to be effective co-workers. Mr. Swindall was adamant about the importance of being a contributor to whatever project work was assigned. The students knew that they all needed to carry their own parts of the assignment, that they needed to communicate clearly, and that they must treat one another with courtesy. Mr. Swindall often said, "These are the capabilities that will make you a valued employee."

So this day, the "simulation" was to track the interactive impact of mice population on the barn owl population; it would become very clear to the students how the prosperity of predators and that of their prey are closely linked. Each student team got a square on the floor which was to represent their meadow where they distributed their round markers to act as mice. Then, from above the square, they dropped their coasters which were playing the part of owls. An owl coaster got to "eat" whatever mice markers he landed on. If the distribution of mice was thick, then the owl was eating well and had offspring that added to the owl population. But when the number of owls grew and grew because there was a plentiful food supply, they ate so many mice that the food supply diminished, and, consequently, with inadequate food, the owl population also shrank. There were additional guidelines for collecting data, and the students graphed the data and then analyzed the graphs to predict the populations for several more generations. It was a memorable class period, and the time ended with some lively discussion of how the owls could become more efficient hunters when the mice became scarce, and how the mice might become more skillful at evading their predators.

The semester ended in a flurry of work, tests, grade reports, parties, and special performances. The Hansons were all excited to have an intermission from school, but if asked, they each would have said, Great Expectations had made the experiences at a new school challenging, but also most rewarding! Rachel Mullins closed the term feeling quite gratified by what she and her students had learned during the semester.

Everyone was ready to enjoy the holidays, but Gabe had already heard the serious urgings from his teachers to work toward the mandated tests for seventh graders in math, reading, and geography. He didn't really care about those test scores himself, but they must be important, based on the tension that seemed to permeate the mood whenever "the tests" were mentioned. Jackson wasn't concerned about tests, but he did worry about how his cats were faring back at the old house. He didn't know if the new owners were letting Callie and Big Gray into the garage on the coldest nights. He had campaigned for hamsters for his Christmas present – a good idea, he thought, since the pet store out on the main road had a sign for "Free Hamsters," but he wasn't very hopeful about receiving that kind of gift. Sarah knew the next semester would hold more ACT testing and college applications, but she preferred to think about the special events surrounding the junior-senior banquet and the fact that surely she had to have a new dress. As Rachel left her classroom for the holidays, she thought, "I must be a true teacher now." She had two bags full of "teacher Christmas gifts" to prove it, and she was thinking ahead – even at the start of the mid-year break. "What all can I do for Penguin Awareness Day when school resumes in January?"

"The value of a man resides in what he gives and not in what he is capable of receiving."
ALBERT EINSTEIN

Chapter 5

Consulting with a Coach

"Everything that can be counted does not necessarily count; everything that counts cannot necessarily be counted."
ALBERT EINSTEIN

The new semester began on the heels of the New Year's Day celebrations. For the most part, students and teachers were glad for the fresh start of a term. Rachel was truly happy to see all of her students back at school. The first graders were full of stories about what gifts they'd found under the Christmas tree, and it seemed as if they had all grown a little taller. Mrs. Aransus explained at the first teachers' meeting that their Great Expectations Coach would be coming the second week of January. As Rachel glanced around the gathering of teachers, she saw smiles on all the faces. Betty Webster, the GE Coach who visited their school, was well-liked, and her visits were always helpful.

Rachel had made great strides in her confidence as a teacher and in her efforts to utilize the Great Expectations practices, especially since she was surrounded by the team of first grade teachers who were all generous in giving her sideline tutoring in GE. She appreciated the day she'd gotten to spend at the GE Fall Conference, and the other Lavonia Berber teachers answered questions and gave her examples of how to implement Great Expectations in her classroom on a daily basis. She did remain mindful of her own teaching and whether it would be assessed as exhibiting one hundred per cent of the GE practices. She wanted that distinction since Lavonia Berber was a Great Expectations Model School, and Mrs. Aransus and her fellow teachers aspired to retain that designation, not only so they could fly the GE flag with its insignia of a leafy green oak tree, but mainly because they believed it was what was best for their students.

When Betty Webster arrived, she spent the morning with Mrs. Aransus. The two of them compared the Great Expectations practices with the proceedings in the classrooms and reviewed how the school was operating in the Rise and Shine assemblies, in the cafeteria, in the PE and music classes, in the speech pathology sessions, and, in fact, in every facet of the school. If there were an area that Mrs. Aransus and Mrs. Webster agreed needed work in order for the teachers to be fully implementing Great Expectations, then Mrs. Webster focused on providing resources to help. In some instances, she suggested a book or a website as a reference, or she and Mrs. Aransus just discussed what that practice should look like. "What can I do to help you be accountable to the plan that you've made?" asked Mrs. Webster.

After lunch, Mrs. Aransus and Mrs. Webster took a checklist with them and went to make observations of teachers on the job. Mrs. Webster called the checklist a data collection form; it was a way for the principal to evaluate whether the teachers were fully following all of the Great Expectations practices. Mrs. Aransus made arrangements for Rachel to be gone from her classroom, so that she could accompany them to observe Great Expectations in action in the classrooms of her colleagues.

As the trio moved down the first hallway, they encountered Miss Counts and her fifth grade math students. The students were working in teams to measure the odd-shaped polygons which Miss Counts had marked on the floor with blue painter's tape. Next, the teams were to calculate the perimeter and area for each polygon.

After an exchange of warm greetings, Mrs. Webster said, "Tell us what's happening with your hallway project."

Miss Counts explained how proud she was of the students' work. "They are doing a fabulous job of working together and problem-solving. Oh, and we have a good example of perseverance. Hannah, Evie, and Kayla," she called, "Come tell Mrs. Webster and Mrs. Mullins how you have had to persevere."

"Well," said Hannah, a pretty fifth grade girl with long blonde hair, "we know that the formula for area is length times width, so that was what we were doing."

The girls like to talk so Evie was quick to pick up the story, "Yes, so even on that polygon that is shaped like a big T, we multiplied length times width times the next length times the next width and so on."

"It took us forever because the numbers kept getting bigger and bigger. We came up with an area of 10,752,000 square inches!" said Kayla with some chagrin as she read the number from the paper bearing all their calculations.

"Ten million square inches!" exclaimed Mrs. Webster.

"The answer is actually 134 square inches," said Hannah with a sheepish grin. "But we know mistakes are okay, and we learned from our mistake. Now, we know that we should have just broken the polygon into plain rectangles, calculated the areas of the pieces and then added those amounts. We will never forget how to do the area of an odd-shaped polygon!"

"Never!" exclaimed Kayla and Evie with fifth grade drama.

"And at least we were perseverant, right, Miss Counts?" added Kayla cheerfully.

"You certainly were," said Miss Counts with a smile. She raised her hand and waited. In a moment, students, who saw her hand, stopped talking and raised their own hands and turned their attention to Miss Counts. Very soon, conversation had stopped entirely, and all eyes were on Miss Counts.

Miss Counts said, "Turn to one or two classmates and discuss when a person might need to know the area of an odd-shaped polygon."

While the students were conferring, Rachel quickly labeled the data collection page with check marks for *working in groups*, *using critical thinking*, *learning from mistakes*, *applying life principles*, and *relating coursework to the real world*.

After the students had had time to reflect on the question and brainstorm answers, they shared many possibilities: wall space to be painted, floor area to be carpeted, lawn to be covered with sod, ...

"Tomorrow," said Miss Counts, with contagious enthusiasm, "we will calculate volume to see which prism will hold more popcorn, one made from a sheet of typing paper folded length-wise or one made with the paper folded side-ways."

"Oh," thought Rachel, and she marked "*linking subject to subsequent material*" on her check sheet.

As Miss Counts and her students picked up and prepared to return to their classroom, Mrs. Aransus led the others around a corner and past a doorway where they could hear a recitation from a kindergarten class.

We are Mrs. Wayland's class.
We are smart children.
We will work hard.
We will be kind and polite.
We are good citizens.
We will succeed because
WE CAN!
AND WE WANT TO!

Rachel and the others smiled at the full-voiced enthusiasm that the students used on the closing lines.

"That's the kindergarten class creed in Mrs. Wayland's room," explained Mrs. Aransus. The children recite their creed daily, and Mrs. Wayland uses it when the children need to be reminded to be kind and polite or to stay on task if an assignment seems difficult. She will prompt them to recall their commitment to "work hard." Rachel could really see how student dedication to a creed helped to give them responsibility for their own conduct, and she checked the line on her data collection form that said, "*A school, class, or personal creed is recited or reflected upon daily to reaffirm commitment to excellence.*"

The trio of observers walked by Mr. Moore's first grade classroom; it had a banner above the door that said, "Expect More with Mr. Moore!" Rachel had already seen the January project that Mr. Moore had developed for his students. They made an igloo in their room by using hot glue to fasten together 500 milk jugs. The project provided many opportunities for the students to cooperate and be contributing workers as they rounded up plastic milk containers and made sure they were clean. Their igloo was large enough to hold 8 to 10 first graders during free reading time, and sometimes Mr. Moore would climb inside himself. They did math, science, social studies, and reading topics all related to the igloo. Somehow reading was better in an igloo.

The student work on display in the hallway from Mr. Moore's students was evidently a penguin art project which had allowed for creativity and critical thinking. Like the milk jug igloo, it was a good cold weather assignment having to do with "ice," but the students would all be able to explain that igloos are used in the northern hemisphere, while penguins live in the southern hemisphere. Students used torn pieces of paper in white and black with a little orange for beaks and feet, and then they referred to photos and books on penguins and glued their colored pieces on sheets of blue background to show penguins on ice floes floating in the ocean. Some penguin figures were diving or swimming. The black and white flightless birds were "assembled" quite accurately, for first grade effort, and the variety of poses showed that each student did his or her own decision-making. There was an accompanying map that showed where in the world penguins live. The whole project had been completed in time for National Penguin Awareness Day on January 20.

Mrs. Webster commented that they were observing classroom activities which allowed for students to assume responsibility and for all students to experience success. "It is a rich way to display students' work by posting it in this hallway where everyone in the school passes and sees what students have accomplished." Rachel made three more check marks on the list in her hand.

Mrs. Aransus suggested that it would be a good time to go into Mrs. Beck's classroom. After she knocked, the door was opened by Justin, a dark-haired fourth grader who had had opportunities to "visit" Mrs. Aransus in her office in the past to iron out breakdowns in his conduct. Justin's home life was chaotic. He was often angry and could become verbally aggressive and even physical when he became frustrated.

"Welcome to our Fourth Grade Clerisy," he said. "We, the Intelligentsia of Lavonia Berber Elementary, are glad you are here. My name is Justin Fielder, how may I help you this afternoon?"

Mrs. Aransus introduced Mrs. Webster and Rachel and asked that they be able to visit the classroom. Justin showed them to visitor chairs situated just behind his own seat. Mrs. Beck's class progressed with little notice to visitors in the room. They were wrapping up their discussion of an Aesop's fable, "The Ant and the Dove." In their focus on vocabulary words, they discussed *quench, plucked,* and *perceived.* They matched words and phrases that related to water, trees, and animals in the fable; they concluded with a discussion on cause and effect and the moral of the fable.

Mrs. Aransus didn't realize that she was subconsciously holding her breath as the class members began following Mrs. Beck's instructions to put away their reading and get out their math folders and measuring tapes. Justin, however, was following instructions instead of lapsing into misconduct; it was the classmate nearest him who began converting his tape measure into a sword. Mrs. Aransus knew the situation had the potential to become disruptive; she expected Justin to elbow his neighbor and order him to quit fooling around. Instead, Justin merely leaned over and said, "No bees, no honey; no work, no money!" That was a quotation used often in the class as a positive reminder to stay on task. The other boy gave a startled look, retracted his tape measure, and looked up toward Mrs. Beck. Mrs. Aransus had her own internal celebration, and Rachel could see the beneficial effect of the school's practice of applying quotations to real-life situations; it was a form of guidance, or discipline, really, that the students administered themselves.

Mrs. Webster's comment when the trio returned to the hallway was "Good things are happening in that classroom," and she elaborated on what she had observed: enriched vocabulary, interpersonal communication skills as demonstrated by the visitor greeter, critical thinking, and internalizing life principles.

Mrs. Aransus was pleased that her teachers were carrying on the business of teaching in a way that was benefitting the academic progress of the pupils and also maintaining the climate of respect. "I have to tell you about another example of the life principles at work," she said. "In order to recognize the life principle of honesty in our school environment, we encourage students to bring to the office any item which they find. I've got quite a collection of things from this endeavor, with a preponderance of pencils. Whoever turns in an object is recognized at Rise and Shine on Friday morning for modeling the life principle of honesty. As a side note, many of the students who are seldom recognized in areas such as academics or athletics are particularly diligent in turning in objects on a regular basis. I am so glad that it is a way for them to receive some positive affirmations. Last month there was a high school basketball tournament going on with large crowds every night. Elizabeth, one of our students from a family that often needs financial assistance, found a one hundred dollar bill on the floor near the concession counter; she turned it in immediately. The man who had lost the money soon returned to the concession stand in a panic. He was surprised, but so pleased, when the concession stand faculty members returned his cash. Elizabeth earned praise for her actions, of course, and was featured in the local newspaper with a picture and a story. The story of Elizabeth and the hundred dollar bill has become one of our models for honesty."

"How wonderful!" exclaimed Mrs. Webster. "Honesty may now be a lifelong trait for her and her classmates."

"Do you have time for more classrooms?" asked Mrs. Aransus.

"Just one more," replied Mrs. Webster.

A third grade classroom was their final stop of the afternoon. Students were working on a recitation of memory work, and it certainly met the description of being exuberant and full of expression. Mrs. Aransus and her guests were welcomed to the classroom when they knocked on the door, and they were able to watch students reciting stanzas of Robert Frost's poem "Stopping by Woods on a Snowy Evening."

> Whose woods these are I think I know.
> His house is in the village, though;
> He will not see me stopping here
> To watch his woods fill up with snow.

The students were obviously enjoying their rendering of the poem, and the presence of Mrs. Aransus and her guests heightened their zeal for the performance. They were saying the words from the Frost poem, but at the appropriate time, they held up various literal objects that fit the words or were homonyms for the words they were saying.

For the word "whose" a student held up a poster board with a student drawing of an owl and "*Ho-o-o*" printed several times; "woods" was demonstrated by a student clapping together two small blocks of wood. For "are," there was a sign showing the letter *R*. And each time the word "I" was uttered, a student showed a classmate's drawing of a person's eye. One student pantomimed "house" by holding his arms above his head like a roof, and the "village" was then three students pantomiming roofs. "In" was identified by the letter *N*, "see" was the letter *C*, and "to" was the number 2. For "not" a boy had a rope tied in a knot. They followed the same tactic for the words and phrases in the whole poem. The students thought the best joke was the fact that they had a classmate whose name was Phil, so on the phrase "fill up," Phil did indeed jump up!

It was an entertaining and funny conclusion to the afternoon of observations, and Mrs. Aransus, Mrs. Webster, and Rachel thoroughly enjoyed celebrating with the class at the conclusion of their performance. Rachel marked her chart for *recitation, celebration,* and *word identification skills* because of the homonyms the students had utilized. There had been a good bit of creativity and critical thinking involved in the project, too, because the students had had to come up with what literal objects they could use.

Mrs. Webster had to leave, Mrs. Aransus needed to be in her spot near the front door to tell students "good bye" when the dismissal bell rang, and Rachel had just enough time to go retrieve her students from their music period before the school day ended. She was quite eager to fully implement Great Expectations in her own classroom after her stint of observing, but Nicholas, one of her first graders, seemed to have totally forgotten their procedures for traveling in the hallway. Rachel halted the line, spoke to Nicholas, and asked him to go to the back of the line and follow in that spot to see how all of his classmates were correctly abiding by the procedures.

Moments later, when Rachel glanced back to check on the line and especially to verify Nicholas's behavior, she saw that he was not at the end of the line at all. Feeling a notch higher degree of frustration, she moved back to Nicholas who was walking in the slot next to last, not at the last place as he had been instructed.

"Nicholas, I asked you to walk at the end of the line," she said quietly.

"I know," he said, but without any remorse; and then he added, "she told me to go in front of her." He pointed at Kimber, his classmate who was now walking at the end of the line.

"Kimber," said Rachel, "why did you go to the end of the line?"

"Oh, Mrs. Mullins, you know," said Kimber, her big brown eyes shining, "We will use good manners and allow others to go first."

Rachel could not argue with that! It was Expectation Number Three which she herself promoted every day, and Kimber was committed to living up to her teacher's standards!

> *"Discendo docebis; docendo disces.*
> By learning you will teach;
> by teaching you will learn."
> LATIN PROVERB

It was in the week following Mrs. Webster's visit to Center City schools that the school board hosted a sort of open house at their monthly meeting. There were some student accomplishments to be recognized and some faculty and staff members who were to be spotlighted during the Center City Board of Education meeting.

Lyle and Julie went to the meeting; there had been other opportunities for them to attend, but this was the first time they had been to a board meeting. They met some other parents and were glad to hear some of the favorable comments that matched their own experiences in the school system. Honestly, Lyle and Julie had not witnessed such a culture of respect in the other schools their children had attended, and here at Center City, the businesses and community organizations all seemed to be working together toward common goals of good character.

They met the parents of Gabe's friend, Lowell Brown. "Yes," said Mrs. Brown, "I'm so impressed by the level of language that the students use in their classroom and their politeness. I went to visit Lowell's classroom one day just before Christmas because I had volunteered to help with assembling the donations for Jacob Lambert's family after the apartment fire. I was greeted at the door and welcomed. When I accepted an offer of a cup of coffee, the student prepared it for me and then served me as nicely as I would have been served in a coffee shop."

"Oh, wow!" said Julie. "I'll have to remember that when I'm out and about on the next cold day and need a cup of cappuccino!"

Their conversation was halted with the start of the meeting which included a sort of "State of the School" report from the superintendent. Superintendent Mackie was well acquainted with Great Expectations, and, in fact, he credited the schools' implementation of the practices with much of the success the school system was enjoying. Lyle and Julie were truly impressed with information on the charts the central office had compiled to share with the school board and parents.

"First of all," said Superintendent Mackie, "most of you remember from my previous reports that since we've instituted Great Expectations practices in our schools across the district, we have made very clear improvement in attendance and have attained markedly lower drop-out rates. Also, my principals all report fewer discipline referrals."

Then Superintendent Mackie referred to the charts that had been handed out to those in attendance. They showed that the district grade point average ranked second in the state, and their athletics and fine arts programs had won numerous academic achievement awards from the state's secondary activity association. He also had a chart to show the district's high ranking on students' scores in state-mandated tests. On those same state-mandated tests, Center City had the second highest percentage of students scoring at "advanced level" among peer districts. Superintendent Mackie also noted the impressive number of National Merit Semifinalists at Center City High School, and showed the chart of the rising trend in the ACT college entrance exam scores for CCHS. Clearly, Superintendent Mackie was pleased with the overall standing of the school in all the ways that the state measures a school's academic progress.

Lyle and Julie were well pleased, too. The schools were serving their children well and seemed to promise continued academic success and development in the character traits that would serve them to advantage in the future.

"High achievement always takes place in the framework of high expectation."
CHARLES KETTERLING

Chapter 6

The "Beastly" Month of February

"You are a citizen, and citizenship carries responsibilities."
PAUL COLLIER

It was February; and the folderol of Valentine's Day, the school's teams in basketball playoffs, Sarah's drama production, Lyle's work, and Julie's Internet sales were all on the family's agenda.

It was also Gabe's birthday. As far as he was concerned, that took priority over all the other events. Aunt Becca used one of her many talents to crochet Gabe a hat as a birthday present. He liked hats, had a hat collection, and enjoyed being the guy with a hat; it was a regret of his that hats were not permitted at school. In fact, he knew Principal Wagner was certain to remind any boy who attempted to ignore the "no hat zone" at school to be respectful and remove headgear immediately. That was a dumb part of the dress code in Gabe's opinion. Nevertheless, he couldn't have been more pleased with a gift than he was with the Aunt Becca hat. It was a crocheted Viking helmet with horns AND a long, red crocheted beard that flowed nearly to his waist. After the Saturday family birthday lunch, Gabe – with hat – had pictures taken in numerous poses, then slipped outside.

There had been a little reprieve in the cold weather so the day was relatively pleasant. His scooter was sitting in the garage, and he decided it would be a good time to take a smooth scooter glide down the driveway. He was quite a sight for anyone who glanced outside because there he was hurtling down the driveway wearing a Viking helmet and sporting a red yarn beard flying in the breeze. Adding to his startling appearance was the fact that his pants were lacking a seriously needed belt, so he was holding his jeans in position with his thumbs through the front belt loops. Somehow, he still managed to steer his scooter.

Gabe had made several runs with the scooter, beard, and too-loose pants when his friend Lowell showed up on his bike. Lowell was appropriately impressed with the bearded Viking hat, and he and Gabe made up several versions of a game that involved scooter and bike and a sloping driveway.

They talked about a variety of topics interesting only to seventh grade boys, but then somewhere in the middle of their game and conversation, Lowell asked, "Do you have the poem memorized for Monday?"

"What? You mean that 'I'm Nobody' poem?" replied Gabe.

"Yes, I've got it," said Lowell proudly, "Listen:

> I'm nobody! Who are you?
> Are you nobody, too?
> Then there's a pair of us—don't tell!
> They'd banish us, you know.
>
> How dreary to be somebody!
> How public, like a frog
> To tell your name the livelong day
> To an admiring bog!"

"Cool," said Gabe as he cut some figure 8's with his scooter, "but you said 'live' (lĭv) wrong."

"What do you mean?" retorted Lowell, "It is 'live' (lĭv) like a 'live ball.'"

"No, I'm pretty sure Mrs. Wilson said 'live-long' like 'I will live a long time,'" said Gabe, pulling off his hat and beard and heading to the garage to put his scooter away. He was thinking there might be some bananas they could eat and maybe they had stayed outside long enough for his mom to get the dishes put in the dishwasher. He knew there was no hope of getting any snacks if she was still washing dishes from lunch. "Come on, we can use my mom's computer and look up that website that will pronounce words for us."

The boys used Julie's laptop on the kitchen counter, ate bananas while the machine booted up, and found the pronunciation for "livelong" to be just what Gabe had said: "līv-long."

"Hmmm," said Lowell trying to process the difference in pronunciation. "Okay, if you're sure." He began to practice saying "lĭv-long day, lĭv-long day, lĭv-long day…"

"Now say the whole poem," commanded Gabe, speaking around the bite of apple in his mouth; it was his second piece of nourishment. He had already finished the banana.

Lowell began speaking obediently:

"I'm nobody! Who are you?
Are you nobody, too?
Then there's a pair of us—don't tell!
They'd banish us, you know.

How dreary to be somebody!
How public, like a frog
To tell your name the livelong day…. "

But he once again said līv-long.

Gabe groaned and collapsed on the floor as if he were stricken.

"What?!" exclaimed Lowell.

"You said it again!" replied Gabe.

"Well, mistakes are okay. Isn't that what Mrs. Wilson says?" said Lowell in defense.

"Yes, but the rest of that is 'we learn from our mistakes and correct them,'" said Gabe.

"Well, I did learn from a mistake this morning," said Lowell without a glimmer of distress over the distinction of *līv* and *lĭv*. "Do you know what cumin is?"

"What? No. What is it?" asked Gabe.

"It's a spice that Mom uses in guacamole and – I don't know – Mexican foods. Anyway, I was fixing my own breakfast and accidentally got cumin. That was the mistake, and the lesson is 'Read labels.' Cumin French Toast is not as good as Cinnamon French Toast!"

By Monday when the seventh graders were to recite their Emily Dickinson poems, Gabe had heckled Lowell enough that he actually said "līv-long" when he gave his recitation. Gabe gave him a small "thumbs up," an affirmation from his friend which was the best that Lowell wished for as a celebration of his success. However, Mrs. Wilson had some other plans.

She pulled out a cardboard box overflowing with an eclectic collection of items that might well have come from the trash. Many of the pieces bore slogans including "It's the real thing," "M'm! M'm! Good!" and "You're in good hands." Mrs. Wilson referenced the Golden Globe Awards program at which awards are given for best actor, best actress, best director, and so on. She explained that the students were going to give out awards for categories of their own creation and for which they designed their own "trophies." She demonstrated the idea of the made-up awards by pulling a small lynchpin out of the collection of objects in her box. The fastener was a worn one her husband had used on the drawbar of his old Ford tractor. She showed the lynchpin and explained the important function performed by lynchpins of holding things in place.

"Kyle is extremely good at helping his classmates and teammates stay on task so they can move forward with their projects. He is an essential lynchpin of our class!" she said. And she presented him with the lynchpin she had brought. It was merely an odd piece reclaimed from the hodgepodge of leftover workshop items, but Mrs. Wilson's words made Kyle feel honored, and, of course, the class applauded. That was a nice added bit of recognition.

Mrs. Wilson had the classmates draw names for whom they were to celebrate by creating and presenting an award. "You may use the items from my box, or you may search out and bring from home what suits the award you wish to present." She cautioned that they were to invest their thoughtfulness and creativity, but no money. The assignment was a good one because students had the chance to come up with unique compliments, and the "awards" were special since they were all tailored to fit the recipients. Mrs. Wilson was on hand to ask award-givers questions that prompted truly thoughtful celebrations, and Gabe and his classmates hardly realized they were doing an English class writing assignment combined with a speech assignment.

On the day of the "awards program," each seventh grader was ready with an object to give to the classmate whose name he had drawn and for whom he had written an appreciation speech. There was a tin can presented for a "can do" attitude, a roll of paper towels for a friend who always helped his buddy clean up the "messes" they got into, and a drawing of a bee for the classmate who was industrious about helping others. Riley, who had organized the gathering of items to benefit Jacob's family after the fire, got a chocolate heart wrapped in red foil – candy which was originally purchased for a Valentine's gift – for being a caring person. Gabe was pleased with his award. It was a pickle jar lid from Brianna bearing the slogan "Quality Packed Inside;" he thought it was good to be recognized as a person of quality. The class agreed to give Mrs. Wilson a flashlight battery because she seemed tireless. They told her she "just keeps going and going and going!"

In fact, right after the "awards ceremony," Mrs. Wilson was ready to start the class on some word identification skills by having them learn the roots of a word and then search out other words with the same root.

Michelle's team looked up words that had the root *ped*: *ped*al, *ped*estrian, *ped*estal, *ped*icab, *ped*icure, *ped*ometer, and even *ped*dler. Students could easily catch on to the fact all such words had to do with "foot" or "feet."

Emma's team had the largest collection of words using their root because they searched for words using *hydro*: *hy*droelectric, *hydro*gen, *hydro*dynamic, *hydro*foil, *hydro*plane, *hydro*ponics, and more. The girls on Emma's team were dismayed by the word *hydro*cephalus because they found a distressing picture of a baby whose head was enlarged by the excess of fluid or water in its skull. The boys "helped" everyone remember the definition of *hydro*phobia by providing some demonstrations of how a rabid dog might act.

❧

In Jackson's second grade class, Mrs. Johnson was also working on word identification skills. They had "stepped out" the syllables to a number of the words on their word wall. Then they put together word syllables to create new words for which they made up definitions. Jackson was happy when the class chose his "new" word and definition as the favorite of the afternoon. His offering was "hippogator" which he defined as a hippopotamus with sharp teeth like an alligator. When he told Julie his new word, he proclaimed that he planned to draw a picture showing how such a creature would look.

Jackson and his classmates had added many words to their vocabulary through the year, and Mrs. Johnson was adept at weaving the new terms into her daily conversation with her students. She told them that certain decisions were "within their jurisdiction;" she advised them to work "diligently," and to make sure their conduct was "consistent" with the creed they recited each day. Usually she elaborated on the definition of words she used that were new to her students. "The old bus barn is dilapidated," she said and then added, "that means it is falling down because it needs repair."

But one day, when Justin carried her book bag in to her desk from the hallway, she did not provide a definition when she exclaimed, "Oh, Justin, you are so chivalrous!"

Justin was uncharacteristically quiet in response to her compliment. Mrs. Johnson noticed his thoughtful expression as he squinted up at her.

He was pondering the enriched vocabulary that she fed the class. Finally he asked, "Mrs. Johnson, does your husband understand your words?"

"Most of the time I think he does," she said with a laugh.

When it was time to prepare Valentine boxes, second graders were asked to do that project at home. Jackson fixed a box with an opening large enough to admit not just cards but also gifts of candy. He really was not fond of the task of addressing envelopes on the stack of Valentines that Julie had purchased for his classmates.

"Can I just sign my name and not put names on the envelopes?" he asked.

Julie was running the vacuum sweeper and didn't fully comprehend his question, so she gave him an affirmative answer.

"Yes!" said Jackson, and he did the winner's fist-pump gesture that he had learned from Gabe. He had already signed his name on all twenty-five cards and addressed seven of them. Now he was free of the necessity of writing more names and addresses. His plan was to distribute the seven labeled cards in the appropriate Valentine boxes and then just dump the remaining eighteen cards into whichever box was convenient. He did not think about the possible ramifications when Ella, one of his little girl classmates, received eighteen cards from him!

"Mom," he called. "Now I have to write a Valentine letter to someone I care about. We all turn in our letters for writing credit, and then Mrs. Johnson is going to mail them. I need someone to write to, and I need the address."

Julie suggested letters to Gram, to Aunt Becca, to a cousin, to a friend from their old home town ...

"That's it!" exclaimed Jackson. "I want to write to Callie and Big Gray."

"Your cats?" said Julie with surprise. Jackson hadn't mentioned the cats lately, though she knew he had been distressed by the decision to leave his special pets at their old house with the new owners when they moved. She really didn't know how the cats were faring and felt some trepidation at the thought that the report of the present feline status might not be all that one would hope. However, none of the alternate letter recipients were anywhere near the top of Jackson's list once he had thought of the cats. He labored over his letter for an hour and made sure Julie helped him address his envelope.

"Well," thought Julie, "I don't know that it will mean much to Callie and Big Gray, but his teacher should be impressed with his letter."

Just after Valentine's Day, the area-wide weather shifted to what was suitable for winter. It was cold, and there had been snow enough to cover the roadways. Every teacher and student goes on alert when snow begins falling because it means the following day might be a "snow day" with classes dismissed. It is always difficult for administrators because of the challenge to make up missed days, but no one wants students and faculty to be at risk in their travels to the school building. On this date, however, the snow accumulation was light, and the forecast for the day included temperatures in the forties by afternoon, so the decision was that school would be in session as usual.

Students made their way into the high school building, but they did so with plenty of grumbling. Other schools in neighboring areas had dismissed classes. Some students stayed home, so the general attendance was down. Attitudes were less than best. Mr. Dawson, the high school principal, noted the general malaise among the students as he stood at the front door welcoming the students who were stomping through the snow and leaning into the bite of the chilling wind. Even some faculty members were lacking in their normal cheerfulness.

"What's a principal to do?" he thought. He knew the day would be essentially wasted if a preponderance of the time were spent grousing about "having to come to school." He made some quick plans and calculations, called in the lead teachers for ideas and input, and, just before the first bell, made an announcement over the intercom that students were to assemble in the auditorium. He met them there with a version of "We Will Rock You" playing on the sound system and with an even higher element of zeal than his normal enthusiasm for the students and their studies. When the students were in place, he spoke into the microphone with passion.

"Ladies and gentlemen, I know that it is cold and snowy, and some of us would have welcomed extra time under the covers in our own beds this morning. But this is a school day! We are here to seek excellence – every day! At Center City High, we don't settle for mediocrity. We have important business. If you don't believe you can learn something today or help someone else who is here today, you should go home – now!"

He paused and looked at the students with fervent eyes. The assembly was perfectly quiet.

"Good!" he said. "You are dismissed for first hour class which will start in eight minutes." His band director turned on a recording of "Stars and Stripes Forever" and cranked up the volume. His tactic had transformed the general attitude of the whole student body. He called the teachers aside as they were heading out of the auditorium with students, and his words were still intense.

"Make sure classes are worth your students' time today!" Teachers nodded their heads in agreement and hurried to their classrooms. Their whole mood had been changed as well. Rather than approaching classes with a lackluster, half-hearted effort, they proceeded with a dose of Mr. Dawson's intensity. The potentially flat and unproductive day had turned into a revitalized quest for impressive learning.

Mrs. Barton, for one, was delighted to be at school. It was only a week and a half until the presentation of the drama production she was coaching. It was not a time that she wanted students to miss final rehearsals. She, herself, was operating with a specially renewed enthusiasm for the work she was doing. She had been a drama coach at the school for almost twenty years, and she had a long list of student actors for whom she held special affection. She kept track of their names and the years of their graduations based on her memory of what plays they had performed in.

For Valentine's Day, she had sent a Facebook message to one of her former students because it was his birthday. She didn't remember everyone's birthday, but a student's having a birthday on a holiday made an easy reminder. She hadn't given the birthday greeting much thought at the time, but a day later she received a message back from the student. He wrote, "Hi, Mrs. Barton, thank you! I can't believe you remember my birthday! It seems like just yesterday that I was a fifteen year old in one of your plays. You mean more to me than you realize. I made some very bad decisions in my life after I left school. In fact, I got involved in drugs, and really, one of the main things that kept me from ending up in the gutter, literally, is knowing how disappointed you would be in me if I didn't get straightened up. Thanks for caring, then and now. Love, Stephen." Such a note gave her a wonderful affirmation, but more than that, it bolstered her resolve to uphold standards of good character for the students currently under her tutelage.

The show that Mrs. Barton's thespians were rehearsing was the Commedia del Arte play for which Sarah had volunteered. Sarah did assume backstage duties only. Her friend Melissa was playing the role of Columbine and looked striking in her white dress costume with her dark hair fluffed to curls and intertwined with little flowers and colorful ribbons. Columbine in the play was a mute. Her onstage actions were matched with sound effects which Sarah produced offstage using an assortment of rhythm band instruments: a triangle, wood blocks, a slide whistle, sand blocks, maracas, bells, and finger cymbals. When Columbine tossed an apple in the air, Sarah used a slide whistle to coordinate with the apple's movement up and then down. When Columbine pantomimed knocking on a door to get the attention of another character on the stage, Sarah struck the wood blocks together. Essentially, for every one of Columbine's actions, Sarah did a sound effect. The cast had been practicing the whole show diligently, and Sarah was confident in her mastery of all the sound effects.

Along with the excitement of the nearing production, when Sarah got home, her mom had a report that topped Sarah's exhilarating drama news. Eric had called and left a message for her. Eric was from their old hometown, and in Sarah's mind he qualified for "Most-Prized Date." He was tall and broad-shouldered, and he had a ready smile. He was a senior last year, so now he was a "college man," which fact made him even more appealing. The Hansons were well-acquainted with Eric and his family and had been in the hometown crowd at the old school cheering his success on the football field many times.

"Eric Ellison called this afternoon," said Julie, knowing the news would be a thrill for Sarah. "He will be in Center City next Thursday evening, and he asked if you might like to go with him on a date for supper out at the Grand Inn."

"Eric Ellison? The Grand Inn? Can I go?" said Sarah without taking a breath.

"Well, you need to double-check with Dad, but I think we approve Eric. What about your school obligations on Thursday? Don't you have drama rehearsal?"

The reminder about rehearsal did cause a lurch in Sarah's high octane excitement, but only momentarily. Her rationalization for why she could miss that one practice set in immediately. It was, after all, only a rehearsal. She was not even a character who appeared on stage. Her part was merely knocking around on an assortment of children's noisemakers, besides which, Mrs. Barton, the drama coach, was totally cool. Sarah had her cues all memorized exactly and knew every move of Melissa's that needed a sound effect. All she would have to do is explain that she would be present for the performance, but that she needed to miss Thursday night's practice.

With Lyle's approval of the plan, Sarah accepted the invitation when Eric called back later that evening, and her thoughts shifted to what she should wear. It was a worthy occasion; "Maybe Mom will take me emergency shopping before next Thursday," she thought.

At school the next day, Sarah couldn't wait to tell Melissa the news and describe how much Eric fit the label of a true dreamboat! As Melissa listened to Sarah gush, she was happy for her until she heard the part of the news about Sarah's missing drama practice.

Melissa's eyes widened, "Sarah, you can't go on Thursday night. That is Commedia del Arte rehearsal. How can I be Columbine without your sound effects? You do them perfectly! I'll be completely thrown off if I don't have the sounds at exactly the right time."

"Oh, someone else can fill in for me for that one evening," said Sarah trying to remain optimistic. "I'm going to go talk to Mrs. Barton right now."

Sarah found Mrs. Barton backstage inspecting costumes to make sure everything was ready for the upcoming show. "Hi, Sarah, how's our adept sound effects specialist?" she said with a smile.

"Oh, I'm fine thanks! Mrs. Barton," she began. Mrs. Barton could tell from her intonation that Sarah had more to say.

"Yes, Sarah," said Mrs. Barton. She paused in her work with a fluffy white ruff collar from one of the costumes and gave Sarah her full attention.

"Mrs. Barton, I came to tell you that I won't be at practice on Thursday night." She saw Mrs. Barton's usual smile replaced with a look of worry. "Someone else can just fill in for me, and I'll be back for the show on Friday night."

"Is there some emergency?" asked Mrs. Barton.

"No," Sarah began to feel less sure of her plan; evidently Mrs. Barton placed more weight on her presence at the practice than Sarah realized. She tried to explain that she had a very special opportunity, but evidently supper out with a handsome college guy at the classiest restaurant in town did not fit any of Mrs. Barton's adequate reasons for missing practice.

Mrs. Barton took Sarah to a backstage bench where they could sit down, and she began explaining why it would not be acceptable for Sarah to be gone. First of all it was dress rehearsal. The performance for an audience was the next night. "Though you are not on stage, your role is crucial. Entrances, exits, lines, actions, reactions… all are cued by your sound effects. They have to be placed exactly right. You work beautifully with Columbine; you know Melissa depends on you. It is not something a substitute can do accurately. If any one of the cast is not at dress rehearsal, we cannot present the stellar performance we want on show night. Don't you remember the guideline requirements I gave when we first started work on this project and my call for commitment to be at practices?"

"Yes, ma'am," she said, although she really had not paid attention to those guidelines at all.

Mrs. Barton was still speaking, "Sarah, please reconsider. You are an essential part of the cast; Melissa is counting on you, your fellow cast members are counting on you, and I am counting on you. What does your class creed say about integrity?"

Sarah couldn't look Mrs. Barton in the eye any longer. She said a piece of the creed, "We will always be people of integrity."

"Hmmm," said Mrs. Barton, and then she just waited.

"I'll be here for dress rehearsal, Mrs. Barton. I'm sorry for almost letting you and everyone down."

"Thank you, Sarah," responded Mrs. Barton with a big hug. "If the college guy who asked you out is a young man of good character, he will support your decision for upholding your commitments."

At home that evening, Sarah had to call Eric Ellison and cancel the date. She explained her obligation and the necessity for rescinding her acceptance of his invitation. She was hoping that he would offer an alternative occasion, but he didn't. In fact, he did not even seem disappointed and there was an edge of coldness to his voice.

"No problem," he said. "See you around." Sarah heard the phone click off. He had not even said "good-bye."

"See you around," she thought bitterly. That meant nothing; he didn't even live in Center City. When would she ever "see him around"?

She stomped upstairs to her bedroom, and that's where Lyle found her thirty minutes later. She was sitting in the dark.

"Hi, Honey," he said coming in and sitting on the edge of the bed beside her. "Mom told me about the schedule conflict that caused you to cancel your Thursday night date. You sacrificed what you wanted at the moment in order to honor your commitment. That takes toughness. Way to go! I'm proud of you." And he gave her a dad hug. "Besides, I'm looking forward to the play on Friday night!"

"When Columbine runs across the stage at the end, makes a leap, and is caught by the hero, the cymbals crash is me!" she said smiling through the tears that still stood in her eyes.

Mrs. Barton herself was already thinking about the next issue to be solved by the day of the performance. She was glad that Sarah was present at dress rehearsal to meet all the sound cues, but she had had a student added to her drama roster just two days earlier. His name was Brayden, and although he was old enough to be a senior, he had only barely enough credits to be classified as a sophomore. She had gotten some of his background information from Principal Dawson. He'd been living in another state with an uncle, and now he had been shunted to his grandparents. It seemed that there was no one who really wanted him, and it was no wonder that his schooling had suffered because of his moves from place to place.

Mrs. Barton's immediate thought was how could she involve him in the drama production at such a late date, but she soon hit upon an idea. She hurried him to the big closet full of costumes, and in no time had him attired as a sixteenth century Italian courtier complete with a purple satin vest, a velvet cape, and a striking hat with a plume. In spite of his weak scholastic background and his uncertain home conditions, he was amiable and willing to wear the unusual clothes that Mrs. Barton offered him. Then she coached him on being the greeter at the front doors of the auditorium, where the drama department's performance was to be staged. On the evening of the show, wearing his costume, he opened the door for each set of audience members as they arrived. He smiled and said the different phrases with which Mrs. Barton had primed him: "Good Evening," "Welcome to Center City High's production this evening!" "How are you?" "Come right in!" He smiled and looked into the eyes of the people he greeted, and the theatergoers all smiled back and viewed him as one of the celebrities of the evening.

The effect of Brayden's welcome to Center City High School and the role he was given, which he was able to fill with great success, set him on just the track he needed. He was welcomed, he was needed, and he was successful. The experience was a wonderful boost to Brayden's self-esteem which had been at a low point. Mrs. Barton didn't know it that night, but the good experience was a turning point for him. He stuck with his schooling from then on and eventually graduated. His classmates were all two years younger than he, but there were none of them happier than Brayden the night of the graduation commencement program.

At the cast party after the Commedia Del Arte performance, Brayden was welcomed along with the actors, actresses, back stage crew, and the sound effects technician – Sarah! The show was a success. Mrs. Barton was smiling with an even broader smile than usual, and Sarah realized it had been a blast doing the curtain call. At the refreshment table, Sarah came face to face with Sam Goodwin. He was the speech-maker from Mrs. Baker's government class who had so impressed Sarah last fall with his speech on responsibility. She could even quote some of his guidelines: "If you open it, close it," "If you turn it on, turn it off," "If you borrow it, return it," and "If you make a mess, clean it up."

"Good job on the sound effects!" he said smiling at her and offering that she go ahead of him in the line for food.

"Thanks!" she said. "New Rule: If you sign up to do the sound effects, then strike the triangle and ring the bells when you are supposed to!"

Sam looked at her more closely. What she had just said made no sense to him, but he thought he might like to get to know her better, and Sarah, for her part, was glad that she had upheld her obligation instead of missing dress rehearsal as she had been tempted to do. With Sam Goodwin standing beside her and helping her reach the plate of cookies, somehow missing out on Eric became less of a disappointment.

❦

February seemed to end abruptly since it was a shorter month. When Jackson got home on the last Friday of February, he spotted a piece of mail propped up on the counter in the kitchen where the day's mail was usually sorted. It was addressed to him, and the return address was from their home in the old town.

"Is this for me?" he asked.

"Yes, it looks like it," replied Julie. "Remember you wrote to Callie and Big Gray in care of Mr. and Mrs. Decker at our old house."

"I was worried about them being too cold. Mr. and Mrs. Decker might not have let them in the garage during the cold weather," said Jackson.

"Open it and see what it says," suggested Julie.

Jackson carefully opened the envelope. He was apprehensive that it would have bad news. The cats might be sick or maybe they had run away. When he pulled out the piece of mail inside the envelope, it was a photo of Callie and Big Gray. They were not shivering in the cold outside; they were not even huddled together in the cold garage; they were snuggled close to one another in the seat of a recliner inside the front room of their old house. Jackson could even see a fire burning in the fireplace in the background of the photo. Mrs. Decker had written a message across the bottom of the photo. It said, "Hi, Jackson, thanks for your Valentine. We have become house guests when it is too cold outside. Love, Your Cats."

> "Character is doing what you don't want to do but know you should do."
> JOYCE MEYER

Chapter 7

Maximizing March

"Resolve to perform what you ought; perform without fail what you resolve."
BENJAMIN FRANKLIN

It was time for one of the Center City High Huddles, which were occasions when the whole high school student body assembled in the auditorium for celebrating accomplishments, announcing events, honoring individuals, strengthening students' kinship with one another, and affirming their dedication to attaining excellence.

The agenda for these gatherings varied, but usually, like today, there was some powerful upbeat music playing as the students entered the auditorium and found their seats. The music helped create a mood of happy energy and allowed students to speak to one another as they moved without there being a noisy jumble of voices. Everyone knew the time allotted for the assembly was short, so the groups moved to their seats promptly. Responsibility for planning and presenting the program rotated through an assigned schedule comprised of different school groups including classes, student council, and various clubs. Sponsors of the particular presiding group of the day approved the program agenda. Since different ones created the plans for each assembly, there was an appealing variety in the programs.

The senior class was in charge this week. Sam Goodwin made the announcements of upcoming events, and then he called for the crowd to "raise the roof" in honor of the eight people he named as having birthdays during the week. The birthday honorees stood up; Sam said, "Ready…" The students and teachers held up their hands palms up, and when Sam said "go," they gave three pushes upward as if they were pushing up the roof. The accompanying verbal sound effects were varied; some sounded definitely ape-like, but it was student choice and a liberating change of pace from the diligence they had been pouring into studies all morning.

Sam said, "We hope those of you with birthdays this week have no ceiling to the fun of your celebration or to what you can accomplish in the year ahead."

Tyler, the senior class president, took over with a Making a Difference Award. Most weeks there was some recognition of individuals who had shown kindness to someone, who had contributed to the workings of the school, or who had given a helping hand when it was needed. The recipients whom Tyler announced for the week were a dozen of the boys from the junior class. One of their classmates, Ronnie, had been diagnosed with a brain tumor. Fortunately, the surgery to remove the tumor had been successful, and it was found to be benign; however, he had not been able to attend class for several weeks. The twelve classmates were following part of their junior class motto which stated, "We will not leave anyone behind." Each week two students – a different two each week – met with Ronnie to make sure he knew the assignments and what was going on in classes. They took him the books, papers, and notes he needed, and occasionally a whimsical gift from one of the girls.

Tyler announced the names of those junior classmates and explained their actions. "We honor you for making a difference. You have shown that you are not going to leave a classmate behind." Tyler quoted Ralph Waldo Emerson saying, "The purpose of life is not to be happy. It is to be useful, to be honorable, to be compassionate, and to make some difference that you have lived and lived well." Finally, he handed the honorees each a candy bar, but the best part of the award for those junior boys was the applause from the student body and the faculty. A bonus benefit of the presentation was the creation of a subtle resolve in the minds of other Center City High students who began pondering how they might also "make a difference" and be recognized in some upcoming CC High Huddle.

Three senior girls stepped up next. Earlier they had consulted Principal Dawson for his approval and input and had gotten some funding from the student council to pay for their gift idea. This morning they had invited bus drivers, cooks, custodians, and the school secretary to come to the Huddle. They introduced their special guests and proceeded to tell the startling yearly totals for miles of bus route driven, acres of school buildings cleaned, number of lunchroom meals served, and number of phone calls answered by the school's support staff. In fact, it had been an interesting math challenge coming up with the calculation of those totals. The girls handed out buttons which they had created using the cheerleaders' button-making machine. The buttons read "B. E. S. T." The presenters explained those letters stood for Best Educational Support Team. They sweetened the honor by also presenting coupons to pay for suppers at a restaurant in town. There were truly happy school support staff workers when the B.E.S.T. honorees left the auditorium to a standing ovation from the whole assembly of high school students.

An orderly conclusion to the Huddle followed the announcements of upcoming events, and the students headed to the next hour class accompanied by an elegant piece of classical music that sent them out on a grand note to tackle the high expectations which had just been reiterated for them.

※

One set of students who were likely to be honored for making a difference in the upcoming weeks were part of a service project committee from Mrs. Baker's Government and Politics class. They had taken on what they called "trash abatement." Mrs. Baker helped them schedule a day for picking up trash along the streets leading to the school building. February's snow had finally melted from the ditches, revealing the rubble which had collected over the winter: wrappers, cans, papers, plastic bags, lightweight flower pots blown by the wind, chunks of Styrofoam, and odd items which had made their way to the roadside with no good explanation of how. Mrs. Baker allowed them one period out of her class and joined them herself wearing extra layers of clothing to ward off the cold of the gusty north wind.

Donning orange safety vests and then riding in a small school shuttle bus to their work sites, the class members were easily able to fill their plastic bags with collected litter and leave the roadsides looking much improved. They even had time to wash their hands and have hot chocolate and cookies before the class period ended. It was a worthy project because unsightly trash truly needed to be cleared from the streets near the school, and the student workers' pride in their accomplishment led to a consciousness of the detrimental impact of littering for future days.

Mrs. Baker viewed the project as a way to explain social responsibility to her government students, as well as a great means of emphasizing their obligation as individuals to act for the benefit of society. She also appreciated the fruits of her class discussion on social competence and building empathy for others. She had observed one excellent example. As the students formed impromptu teams and climbed off the small bus, Sam Goodwin turned to Trenton and said, "Come on, Trenton. We can be partners."

For however popular Sam was, Trenton was the opposite. He had a tough background, could not read well, and usually wore a shabby brown work jacket and camo pants. He was clearly surprised that Sam had invited him, of all people, but the two of them worked hard and made a good team. Mrs. Baker was impressed with Sam's willingness to bolster someone else's sense of worth, and meanwhile Trenton stored up the good feeling of being accepted and of being a contributor to the project effort. In fact, it was the good experience on the trash abatement project that later led Trenton to sign up for EMT summer training with the local volunteer fire department. Sam had made a difference that day in more than one way.

※

Sarah wasn't part of the trash abatement project; instead, she was studying for the upcoming Advanced Placement tests. She felt as if she was ready for the English Lit and Composition test. Last week, Mrs. Trotter had the AP class assemble portfolios of the best pieces of their writing from the whole year. She had helped Sarah and each of her classmates look at their own past performance and judge how far they had come. Mrs. Trotter's strategy for putting student work on display, for this occasion, was to leave the portfolios at the offices of various prestigious professionals in town: doctors, lawyers, dentists, and optometrists. The portfolios went in the waiting room areas for patients and clients to read; Mrs. Trotter had even inserted comment pages so the AP students would receive feedback from their "readers." To Sarah and her classmates, it almost felt as if they were published authors; they looked forward to retrieving their portfolios and seeing the comments added to their notebooks.

Sarah was also in Advanced Placement German Language. Mr. Zimmerman used flexible grouping as the class prepared for their tests. He started with the class working as a whole group on the portion of the test covering authentic print materials such as journals, literary texts, announcements, advertisements, letters, maps, and tables. This part of the review he conducted with his "classroom response system." Students read the printed material in front of them; Mr. Zimmerman posted a multiple choice question on his interactive whiteboard; and then students submitted their answers with handheld transmitters called clickers. The transmitters sent signals to the receiver which was attached to Mr. Zimmerman's computer. The software on his computer collected the student answers and showed him immediately how many students had answered correctly. He liked the technology because it gave him an accurate and immediate picture of how well the students were doing. He could tell which questions needed additional clarification. He was also pleased with being able to electronically save the review questions that he had displayed so he could email the material to students who missed class because they were attending at least one of the special events that crowd the calendar in the spring semester. On the students' part, the exercise was engaging because each student was called upon to answer every question.

Before Mr. Zimmerman acquired his response system setup, he had conducted a low-tech version of a similar review with immediate feedback from his classes using squares of red, orange, and green construction paper. He would read a question, students marked their answers on their papers, and when Mr. Zimmerman provided the correct response, he asked students to show their status by holding up a green card for a correct answer, a red card for an incorrect answer, or an orange card for a correct answer but one needing clarification. He found it useful to be able to tell at a glance if the whole class had a good understanding of a question or not. He could also track individual students to judge how well they were doing on the review. He could respond efficiently to any class content that needed re-teaching.

After work with the class as a whole, he divided the students into small groups for listening to authentic audio materials including interviews, public service announcements, and conversations. Then the members within each group could discuss the content and come to a consensus on the answers related to the material they had just heard. Mr. Zimmerman grouped students that had common needs so he could maximize the time he used to coach them on weak areas.

Finally, Mr. Zimmerman asked the students to work individually in preparing for the writing and speaking portion of the test. They needed to do some research in order to be able to write a persuasive essay and be ready to give an oral presentation in response to a prompt on a cultural topic, all using the German language that they had been studying. Mr. Zimmerman's tactics were a smooth application of the Great Expectations practice that indicates learners are to be taught thoroughly and to mastery, insuring success for all with whole group instruction being interwoven with flexible group instruction and individual instruction.

Sarah still had studies that were keeping her busy in math class. She enjoyed Mr. Dobbs and had developed a competition with him. The challenge was to see which one of them could utter the words, "Good Morning" first when they met in the hallway each day. Mr. Dobbs nearly always won. Sarah's comment to her dad about Mr. Dobbs was that he was like a salesman. Whatever topic they were covering, he spoke to them about why they needed to understand the concept, why they wanted it, how it was valuable, and where they would use it in the future. Mr. Dobbs often explained the practical application of the math functions they were studying.

On March 14 or 3/14, Mr. Dobbs livened up class with some Pi Day activities in honor of the mathematical constant (pi) which has 3.14 as the first three digits of its decimal form. Though the class might have preferred having pie to eat like they did last year, this time, Mr. Dobbs challenged them each to draw a picture incorporating the π symbol. While they worked on their sketches, Mr. Dobbs hung a poster of Albert Einstein, whose birthday was March 14. The short design project took only a small portion of the class period, but it promoted math, helped everyone remember 3.14, and especially appealed to the students' visual-spatial talents.

The students who finished their pi drawings and also had their homework assignments completed were sent to an online math program to continue at their own pace in studying the topic they had been covering in class. The program gave them problems to work, and as they correctly completed questions and solved challenges related to the class concepts, they could move forward to the next tier of equations and math functions. The program had problem generators on many different topics, and if a student was struggling, he could ask the program to show him a step-by-step solution. It was a great way for Mr. Dobbs to offer individualized instruction, and for some students, it was an ideal avenue for accelerating their understanding and mastery of math concepts. Sarah liked the opportunity to challenge herself, and since it was a free program online, she could also practice material at home. She was certain it was going to help her be more successful with her college course work next year.

~~

By the time Sarah got home on Pi Day, Jackson had already been there nearly an hour. He was happy that daylight savings time was in effect so there would be more time outside before it got dark. As a bonus, it was a sunny day and much warmer weather than they had been experiencing. Julie was immersed in preparing items to mail that she had been able to sell online: a 1900's brass egg lifter, a set of rabbit-shaped cookie cutters, a glass cornstick baking pan, six vintage travel postcards, three Nancy Drew novels, and a set of black stone earrings. When Jackson came through the dining room where Julie was working with packaging materials spread out across the table, a large star ornament caught his eye. It was at least two feet across; it was made of pierced tin and was designed to be illuminated by a whole strand of Christmas lights that were attached inside.

"Mom, Mom, Mom," he said excitedly. "Can I have this?"

It was lying on top of a box of decorations which Julie had purchased for just one special oil derrick Christmas ornament. She'd sold the derrick ornament for a hearty sum, but she really had no expectations of selling the star. "Sure, if you want it," she answered.

Jackson proceeded to commandeer help from whichever family members he could find. He asked Sarah to help him get the outdoor power cord that would reach from an outlet at the front of the house halfway down the driveway. He persuaded Gabe to move the tall stepladder from the garage out to the driveway. Then when Lyle got home, Jackson requested his help in tying the star up using a line that stretched between two trees and suspended the star up over the driveway. When it got dark, he would be able to plug in the power cord and have a lighted star.

Of course the family wanted to know why he thought of doing such a thing, and he was happy to give his full explanation. The second graders had been studying France for international studies throughout the year. They learned about French history, language, culture, traditions, fashion, foods, games, and landmarks. Today, Mrs. Johnson had shown a video of a beautiful area in southeastern France. For one small village, there was a gold-painted star hanging on a long chain suspended between two cliffs above the town. The narrator of the film retold the legend that the first star was hung over the village by a knight when he returned from the Crusades. That had been in the 10th century. Through the years, the village has replaced the emblem whenever it fell.

Jackson had been intrigued by the suspended star, and then at home when he saw the star ornament in Julie's stash of garage sale purchases, it occurred to him that he could hang a star himself. With the help of his crew of family members, Jackson had his star dangling above the driveway before supper.

"Good job on the star!" said Julie.

"That's 'cause I am tenacious!" replied Jackson proudly. Lyle and Julie were proud as well, but they were not willing to promise that the star would be maintained above the driveway as long as the famous one that has dangled high above the French village, Moustiers-Sainte-Marie, for centuries.

At sunset, the family went outside to watch while Jackson plugged in the power cord to light his star. The star's spectral glow gave Sarah inspiration for an assignment that was due in her English class by the end of the week. After an interesting discussion of urban myths, which the teacher called modern folklore stories told as an experience of a friend of a friend, Mrs. Trotter had asked the class to create new urban myths as a writing assignment. Students were to take pictures of the settings of their myths and then write the stories. Sarah wasn't sure just how her fanciful story would turn out, but the glowing star, seeming to float above the driveway, was most certainly going to be an element of her newly created legend.

Gabe was interested in the star because of the seventh grade geography that had been on his study list all year. Not only could he tell where France is, but he could also draw a map of Europe and name all the countries. In fact, that assignment sounded easy at the moment because he and his classmates had, most recently, been working to learn all the names of the over fifty countries in Africa. Mr. Lorrie had started them with a map of Africa that had only the outlines of the countries and asked them to fill in what they already knew. Gabe could name Egypt because of Bible class, and he knew of

Madagascar and Morocco though he couldn't point to them on a map. His classmates were similarly lacking in African geographic knowledge.

That did not deter Mr. Lorrie, however. He started the students learning the names of eight countries a day. They began at the top and worked their way around the continent counter clockwise, each day reviewing the countries from the day before and adding eight more. They practiced while the classmate whose turn it was to take role recorded attendance in Mr. Lorrie's computer. Soon the list of countries they could name and locate on the map was growing. Mr. Lorrie used a laser pointer to lead the students in reciting the country names. Some days, one of the classmates got to be the "laser master" and do the pointing. Mr. Lorrie knew from experience with past classes that the seventh graders would soon be able to identify all of the countries. Then, he would give them a blank map again with only the country outlines. Most of the students would be able to label all the countries correctly, and some could start with just a blank page and draw in the country shapes themselves before they added the name labels.

૭∞૭

As the school year advanced to the last half of March, things were progressing well generally at Center City Middle School, but Principal Wagner was cognizant of the undesirable attitude of basic apathy and disrespect that was still present in a small percentage of the CCMS students. He actually counted himself and the school most fortunate because the vast majority of the students were outstanding individuals who conducted themselves in a positive and productive manner. Those young people had supportive parents who echoed the standards that the school promoted. But the small remnants of students who had started with disrespectful attitudes and had begun the school year by holding themselves outside the general community of the student body were still ones that Mr. Wagner observed, hoping to find what they needed for "buy-in." He wanted them to strive for academic excellence and for living in a culture of respect. He had found the best way to deal with this issue had been with the ongoing development of positive relationships with both the students and their parents or guardians. The librarian had been a valuable ally in that effort. She made the library a haven for students to hang out before school and during lunch period. She listened, shared, advised, and encouraged with unflagging patience and a good deal of humor. The positive rapport she had built over the year was proving to be extremely effective in defusing student disruptive and disrespectful attitudes. He counted that librarian as a particularly valuable ambassador for working with the tribe of students who had begun the year as outsiders. Some of those students who had had problems with teachers or classmates had gone through the process of learning a better way and were much stronger and more reliable and more pleasant students now than they had ever been.

Mr. Wagner continued his practice from the first of the year of being at the front door to greet all 700 students as they arrived each morning. His presence assured that there would be no issues in the area outside the building, and sometimes he was able to wave at parents who dropped off their teenagers. One day, Mr. Wagner was called away, and so he was not in his spot. Kale, a student who had started the year with a surly attitude but had now mellowed to accept the standards that the school upheld, was the one to notice that Mr. Wagner was absent from his spot by the front door. He took the initiative to act as the principal's stand-in. When Mr. Wagner came late to take his place, he caught his breath. "Oh, no, what is Kale doing?" he thought. He feared some inappropriate choices such as those that Kale might have made at the beginning of the year. However, as Mr. Wagner stood and watched, Kale was smiling, saying "Good morning," and generally mimicking Mr. Wagner, but doing so with good nature and effectiveness because the arriving students recognized that he was being Mr. Wagner, Jr. Mr. Wagner counted it as a good day.

As the basketball season came to a close, it was time for the coaches to usher in track season. Coach Crowley handed out pages with training schedules, dates for meets, and information about track and field sectionals later in the season. Gabe was elated. Some good rigorous physical activity was what he had wished for and needed all year long. Lyle had already taken him to buy track shoes; Gabe was sure the sleek shoes with colors labeled as hyper punch and electric green would send him flying around the track for whatever event he was running. Track was also interesting because the team was coed. On the first day of practice, it was raining, so the coach had everyone work inside the gym. Gabe felt a little awkward when he knew some girls were watching him, and he accidentally clonked himself in the chin with a weight. And then when they began running, Lydia sped past him as if he were a slacker. Clearly the girls were going to uphold their portion of the team and push Gabe and the other guys to stretch themselves and their efforts in order to win their spots in the competition.

Though the team quickly adopted the mind-set of competitors, and they wanted to be winners and outdo runners from other schools, Coach Crowley helped them keep their perspective of how they should treat one another and their opponents. He also matched athletes with the events for which they were best suited, so soon each of them was feeling a growing sense of competence. With Coach's pep talks and locker room signs, they began to enjoy the camaraderie of being a team in which each of them felt as if he or she mattered. The end result was that the group was made up of individuals who were highly motivated.

Coach took note of the factors that had produced such good motivation for the track team and tried to get the same feelings of competence, belonging, and usefulness in place for the students he had in the state history class he taught. He wanted history students who were as motivated as his track team members.

❧

At Lavonia Berber, besides the consideration of motivation, the teachers continued to ask, "What do my students need to know and be able to do?" It was a consideration that shaped their lesson plans every day. Roger Lewin's quotation: "Too often we give children answers to remember rather than problems to solve" was on Mr. Hardner's mind as he devised some hands-on math assignments. On a warm afternoon, he took his fourth grade class outside for an experiential learning activity. They were to run some experiments to help the learners understand the concept of inertia.

The class was divided into teams, and each team was given a bucket of objects of various sizes, shapes, and weights. They had already had class discussions on how to cooperate in a team and how each member was to fulfill his role, and they could readily quote, "The boat won't go if we don't all row."

Mr. Hardner challenged their thinking; he observed that the students had grown comfortable in holding only minimal expectations of themselves. He asked them to work outside their comfort zones. Each team had an area where the participants could throw the objects from their bucket and observe the path of motion of the things they threw. They recorded their observations, and then they returned to the classroom where they discussed Newton's first law of motion, that an object in motion will stay in motion in a straight line unless acted upon by an unbalanced force. The thrown objects would only go so far before the force of gravity started to act upon them, resulting in a distinctive curved flight path. Their experiment also demonstrated Newton's second law, force equals mass times acceleration. The heavier objects went higher and farther, as did the objects that were thrown faster.

Back inside the classroom, they wrapped up the class period with an application of Newton's Laws of Motion to baseball. They talked about how the laws affect how far a ball will fly when it is thrown or hit, how gravity pulls a ball down, how the acceleration of the ball is caused by the force of the bat, and how cleats compensate for the equal and opposite reaction to the motion of throwing the ball. Besides appropriating the benefit of the ardent interest of the Little League ballplayers in the class, this discussion was most apropos because opening day for the professional baseball leagues was coming up soon. Additionally, it integrated well with "Casey at the Bat," an old baseball poem, which they had discussed in language arts class that morning.

Also, at the elementary school, the second graders were studying for a spelling bee coming up the first week of April. When Julie looked over Jackson's study list of spelling words, she was surprised to note he had shortened his name when he wrote it on the page.

"Jackson," she said, "I thought you liked your name."

He replied, "I do, Mom!"

"Then, why have you signed this paper 'Jack' instead of 'Jackson'?"

"Well, it is in cursive."

"Yes, I see that," said Julie. "And it looks very impressive. You did a good job."

"Yeah, well, we are only up to the letter r, so I can't do Jackson yet. We haven't learned to do s."

"Okay," she laughed, "You can be Jack for a day or two."

Just before spring break, Mrs. Johnson made arrangements for the second grade class to go to the newest educational classes offered at the history museum in town. Jackson's classmates had been to the museum before, but this was the first trip for him since he was new to the school this year. He was excited. Besides a trip away from school, there was the promise that they would get to take special sack lunches.

"So what's this museum like?" he asked Gavin, who was his seatmate on the bus.

"It's pretty neat!" replied Gavin. "Last year, the lady showed us how to make a buffalo out of clay. Then we got to take what we made home. Oh, yeah, and we made dolls out of corn husks, and we all got to try to play American Indian musical instruments. There were flutes and drums, but I got to wear turtle shell rattles on my legs and play them by stomping my feet. They were cool except the ones I wore were not real turtle shells; the Indians used real turtle shells when they made theirs."

Mrs. Johnson enjoyed taking her students to the museum. There were always interesting exhibits for her students to see, and the learning modules presented by the museum staff taught history and were also invitations for students to use their imaginations. Furthermore, there always seemed to be some tie to music and art appreciation.

As much as Mrs. Johnson and her students enjoyed visiting the museum, the museum staff enjoyed them perhaps even more. The Lavonia Berber kids had high standards of behavior instilled in them from the school's use of Great Expectations and their adherence to expectations for behavior and the GE Life Principles. The museum staff knew from the school's trips in previous years that the group would be courteous visitors to the museum.

Last year, Mrs. Johnson had even shown the museum presenter that she could hold her hand up to form the letter c, and the students would follow that signal as an indicator that they should speak in complete sentences. The museum presenters were impressed.

One of the museum docents told Mrs. Johnson that the personnel at the museum could tell when the bus pulled up in front of the building that the students were from a Great Expectations school. They disembarked from the bus in an orderly manner, were not overly boisterous as they toured the exhibit space, and minded the guidelines for protecting the artwork and exhibit pieces. Also, the students' adoption of the life principle of courtesy made them cooperative scholars in the museum's learning modules. When the bus left at the end of their visit, there was no trash strewn around the museum or the grounds. These good behaviors were not apparent in all the school groups that came to the facility.

The museum trip had been a novel break from schoolhouse routine for Jackson and his classmates, and Jackson had been excited about the trip. But an even greater pleasure was on tap for Jackson over Spring Break. Mrs. Stevens, the fifth grade teacher, who kept a rotating menagerie of animals in her classroom, had visited with Jackson enough to know that he was a young person who held special affection for animals. The set of animals in her room changed through the year and included goldfish, hamsters, tarantulas, birds, lizards, turtles, bunnies, and even a pair of ferrets for a short while. Mrs. Stevens, like Jackson, had a high level of empathy for animals. She always had plans for feeding, caging, and caring for the critters that she brought to the classroom.

The animals provided many real life applications from daily lessons. For math, there were calculations on costs of foods as well as on the area a particular animal needed in its cage. Science studies of habitat made more sense when related to their own small zoo, and geography came into play when Mrs. Stevens brought in a Peruvian guinea pig.

Besides the added interest the animals provided in the classroom, Mrs. Stevens saw them as a way to allow students to develop their capability to handle responsibilities. Students came to understand that the animals were dependent upon them, and it was not okay to shirk one's duty to feed and water animals. Students knew the classroom assortment of creatures depended upon them.

Jackson didn't know that Mrs. Stevens had already called his mom and obtained parental clearance before she spoke to him at the end of school on Thursday just as Spring Break was about to commence. He was beyond excited when he climbed into the car with Julie.

"Mom, do you know what?" said Jackson. He spoke rapidly, and the volume of his voice was several notches louder than was required by Julie's presence right next to him in the van.

"What, honey?" said Julie. She knew his happy news already, but she wanted to give him the joy of telling it.

Then without taking many pauses for breath, Jackson began to tell, "Mrs. Stevens asked if I will take care of the two rabbits out of her classroom during Spring Break. She has pens for them, and she will bring them to our house. Can I keep them? It is just for the week. There are two of them, and they are as soft as Callie and Big Gray! Can I keep them?"

When Julie answered in the affirmative, Jackson continued to discuss all that he had learned about rabbit care, so all the way home, Julie heard about rabbit litter boxes, their usual habit of sleeping during the day, the fact that some rabbits could be trained to walk on a leash if you have a harness…"

Julie had to admit to being impressed with all the details about rabbits and rabbit care that Jackson had already absorbed.

"And," Jackson added with full dramatic emphasis, "Mrs. Stevens asked if I can go with her at the end of the school year when she turns loose the tarantulas and lizards. They can live on their own because they are indigestive to our area."

"Indigenous," corrected Julie, but it was with a smile, because she knew Jackson would do a good job caring for the classroom animals for a week, and she appreciated a teacher who was attuned to his special interest in animals although he wasn't even one of her regular classroom pupils.

> *"The opportunity to do better tomorrow than you did today is a privilege – and a duty."*
> H. JACKSON BROWN, JR.

Chapter 8

Spring Fever and Specials

"What we learn with pleasure we never forget."
LOUIS MERCIER

April began with some "just right" rain showers, and the old 1500's quotation from the English farmer and writer, Thomas Tusser, seemed apropos: "Sweet April showers do spring May flowers." It also started off with some of the silliness of April Fool's Day. Mrs. Johnson, Jackson's teacher, offered the second graders brownies, but when they all wished to share in what she had brought, she pulled back the cover to show a pan with construction paper "brown E's." Though she was a sweet teacher at heart and really did have chocolate brownies to share, she also used the April Fool's joke to talk to her students about puns. They were pleased with her comment that being able to understand puns was the mark of a person with a good vocabulary, so they laughed together about some other tricky sentences: "Why did the bee go to the doctor? Because he had hives." "Why did the pony go to the doctor? Because she was a little horse." "Why are teddy bears never hungry? Because they are always stuffed."

ఞఞ

There was little joking among the high school science students who were to be exhibitors at the Regional Science Fair; however, because they were scrambling to complete preparations. Sarah wasn't going, but her friend Melissa was one of the exhibitors. Melissa had been engrossed in her project, and details about her preparations had spilled over into many of her conversations with Sarah. Mr. Swindall, the science teacher, and the twenty students who would travel to the college campus where the competition was being held were all striving to be well-prepared. They had already been presenters at a district-level science fair for which Mr. Swindall had given clear instructions, with a blend of his guidance and a special challenge to the students to be experimenters. He often spoke to them about what they were learning for the short term of doing well on an upcoming test or preparing for next year and for the long term of developing strategies that would be useful for the rest of their lives.

Mr. Swindall was a passionate teacher; he met students at the door to his classroom every day, looked each of them in the eye, and gave them uplifting greetings. They understood he really cared about each of them. He was generous with his compliments; he might ask a student to help with a step in a lab demonstration and then say, "Oh, thank you, I'm impressed; you have the hands of a surgeon."

As they prepared for the trip to the science fair, Mr. Swindall also did some coaching about how they were to dress for the exhibit day. He always modeled appropriate clothing himself with a starched shirt and a tie as part of his standard attire. He talked with them about how clothing is used by others in assessing a person's personality and character, and, maybe even more importantly, about how one is dressed affects one's own self-image and behavior. Melissa's wardrobe for the day included a new navy blue suit that made her feel like a career woman.

On the day before their departure for the fair, the exhibitors were busy packing their display boards and supplies to be loaded on the activity bus when the intercom came to life with the school secretary's voice, "Mr. Swindall, can you please come to the front office. The delivery truck just left a shipment for you, and it is crowding the office."

Mr. Swindall was puzzled because he was expecting a delivery of a dozen fetal pigs for a dissection lab he had planned later in the month, but he would not have judged that the package would be so large that it could be described as crowding the front office. The class period ended and to honor the secretary's request, he hurried to the office to pick up his box. Melissa and some of her fellow science fair exhibitors were still in the science room when Mr. Swindall came back. He had a puzzled grin on his face and was shaking his head.

"What's up?" asked Josh.

"Well," replied Mr. Swindall, "I ordered twelve fetal pigs – I thought – but I evidently looked at the order form wrong. The shipment that came in is twelve boxes, each with twelve pigs. One hundred forty-four! That's more dissection than my students will do in ten years!"

"If you can't make a mistake, you can't make anything," said Melissa, quoting what Mr. Swindall often told his students.

Cody could quote another of the Swindall sayings, "The gift of the moment and its lessons prepares us for a better tomorrow."

"'The greatest mistake you can make in life is to continually fear you will make one,' by Elbert Hubbard," added Rebecca.

"Okay, I've got it!" said Mr. Swindall, and he and the students laughed. He knew the grossly over abundant supply of dissection pigs was an annoying problem that he would have to correct, but it was clear that his students remembered his coaching about mistakes being an avenue for learning.

The next day at the site for the science fair, the Center City students worked with hurried care to get their exhibit displays all set up. Cody had experimented on making an effective solar energy panel using black trash bags. Sabrina tested different natural products for making ink; her best result came from beet juice. Rebecca had done tests in bread-making, varying the quantities of some of her ingredients. Mr. Swindall had been sampling the results of her experiments over the past couple of weeks, although when she had made numerous batches of goat cheese the year before, he had declined to eat any of her products. David had studied compost-making, and along with display boards which outlined how his work followed the scientific method, he brought a large black plastic barrel filled with some of his compost. His classmates were apprehensive about what smell his exhibit was going to exude, but David was quick to defend his "earthy" smelling compost which was ready for the garden.

Melissa had worked on making cyanotype prints. She was ready to explain that cyanotype is a white print on a bright blue background on cloth or paper treated with potassium ferricyanide and ferric ammonium citrate. Mr. Swindall had helped her acquire the chemicals she needed, and she had made prints of plant leaves, stencils she had cut out, and old photograph negatives. She enjoyed her research about the woman who had first used cyanotype and because of it was called the first woman photographer. She also had some examples of old blueprints because making blueprints was the first use of the process. Melissa's mom had allowed her to block the light from the window of the small downstairs bathroom at her home. It worked great as a darkroom, but she got a few small spatters of cyan blue on the white wall paint that she expected were permanent.

After the displays were all arranged, the students stood next to their exhibits waiting for the judges and other guests of the fair to come by and look over their work. The set of exhibitors across the aisle were from another school. Since there was some time for them all to wait, Mr. Swindall's students began listening to the comments flying between the other students.

"Nice pants," said one of the girls.

The boy she was addressing said, "Thanks, they're new."

Her response was, "Oh, new to you maybe, but clowns have been dressing like that for years." The girl next to her joined her in laughing as if it were a hilarious joke.

The boy who had received the evaluation of his pants was not to be outdone, he replied, "Well, a clown personality is better than some people who have no personality at all."

That comment was evidently uproariously funny to the guys standing near him. Every time one of the students in that group spoke to another of his schoolmates, he put some kind of cutting remark into the conversation. Melissa even overheard one of them commenting on the outfit she had chosen for its "successful career woman" look saying, "Did you see the girl with the blueprint project; she's the one wearing the old lady suit…"

The Center City High students did well with the awards they won that day as a part of the science fair competition, and they were wound up with the elation that comes from successfully completing a challenging event. They shared much laughter on the bus ride home, but the laughter did not come at the expense of one another.

Sabrina was the one to express what they all thought about the rude comments of the students from the other school. She said, "I'm glad that we do not use sarcasm or put-downs at Center City."

"And I'm glad that you won't make fun of a person's mistake of ordering 12 dozen pigs instead of 12," said Mr. Swindall with a smile.

"Well, we won't make fun of you," said Josh, "but I'm glad that we can join you in thinking that it is pretty funny."

How well the students were doing academically was certainly on the minds of the middle school teachers since there were mandated tests coming up soon. The teachers met in data teams who looked over the results of assessment tests. They asked "What do the students know? What can they do?" Then they began to plan how to address any weak areas. "Why are some students behind? Who is behind? What strategies could be used to re-teach concepts?" They knew they needed a "new way" to teach – just the same thing over in a louder voice would not be likely to produce results any different than it did the first time.

Mr. Van Arkel, the math teacher, was ready to address the array of math skills which would be on the seventh grade test. He put up NASCAR posters, brought a couple of celebrity drivers in the form of life-size cardboard cutout pictures which he had finagled from a grocery store when its advertising campaign was finished, and leaned a borrowed chrome wheel outside his door with a "Welcome to the Races" sign. Besides that, he had gone through his own garage and brought automotive tools and car parts to distribute around the room. He put the class in teams which he called pit crews, and they were seated around small blocks of desks so they could see one another and discuss the sample problems they were working for each math concept. When everyone was situated and the assignment had been explained, Mr. Van Arkel called out, "Start your engines!" The students picked up their pencils and watched Mr. Van Arkel until he waved a checkered flag and said, "Go!"

Most of the questions that arose as they practiced the numerous skills they were to have learned as seventh graders were answered by the pit crew members, but Mr. Van Arkel also walked around and visited each group.

"I am the crew chief," he said. "You crew members are doing the work, but you can bet I'll be there if anyone needs a hand." He gave specific feedback so the learners could know if they were on the right track; it was a setting that gave him the opportunity to point out that everyone on the team needs to function. They got useful coaching as well as the powerful learning that comes from teaching someone else. Gabe and Lowell thought the NASCAR decorations made the study seem more like a special event than a review for upcoming tests.

Mr. Nelson, the middle school social studies teacher, still had a remaining big project for the year which he had put on the calendar for April. He chose a topic for which he could rent the traveling museum exhibit on "Westward Expansion," and he applied for a small grant to pay for the loan of the exhibit. A couple of the academic standards he was striving to meet for his students were identifying why people choose to settle in different places and analyzing the causes and effects of change in a place over time.

English teacher Mrs. Wilson also had a project for the middle school students for April; class members were each to write a report with levels of sophistication that matched grade levels. She and Mr. Nelson chose to roll their assignments together so that the reports the students wrote for English class were related to the Westward Expansion topics for social studies. The students had discretionary power to choose their own specific topics to match their personal interests, but they gained the benefit of fulfilling requirements for two different classes by working on one project, and also they enjoyed the synergy that came from the fact that all the topics were related to one another. There were research materials online, of course, as well as many helpful books in the school library, and then Mr. Nelson set up a small lending library of his own personal books including a book with art of the Old West as well as one that had many photographs of Indians, settlers, loggers, and Gold Rush prospectors.

As a culmination of the research, study, and writing, Mr. Nelson and Mrs. Wilson planned an open house so the students could explain to parents and other guests what they had learned from their research. Students again had the latitude to decide themselves how they wanted to display their findings. They could make display boards, prepare a computer slide show, or present a living history version of a historical figure. Gabe chose the living history. One could have predicted that option for him because it involved being up and doing. He probably would not have been able to express how much it meant to him to have the prerogative to do assignments that tapped into his bodily-kinestheic intelligence, but his upward trending grades spoke for him.

Gabe's choice of Westward Expansion research topic was the "Overland Stage Line," a stagecoach and wagon trail most heavily used in the 1860's as an alternate route to the Oregon, California, and Mormon Trails. It cut through central Wyoming. Gabe was most interested in the trail's use by the Overland Stage Company to run mail and passengers to Salt Lake City, Utah. For his living history character, Gabe decided to portray an Overlander named Nat Stein, who was a stagecoach driver on the Overland Trail. Mrs. Barton, the high school drama coach, brought wardrobe boxes filled with costume possibilities for the middle school students planning to portray individuals who were significant representatives of the events that were part of Westward Expansion. Mr. Nelson offered Gabe a chance to try on clothes that might serve as his Nat Stein costume and sent him into the custodian closet that opened off the hallway where the seventh graders kept the brooms and dustpans they used for hall clean-up at the end of the school day. Gabe tried on the outfit: baggy pants held up by suspenders, shirt, vest, and a yellow linen duster. They were all over-generous in size for Gabe's slender frame, but they looked like they might have been clothing worn in the 1800's. Gabe locked the door while he was changing because he didn't want someone to come looking for the broom when he was only half-dressed. He came out to show the effects of his wagon driver attire and did not think about the fact that since he had turned the lock button, he would be locked out from this temporary changing room when the door went shut. Mr. Nelson exclaimed over his authentic clothing and added a flat brimmed hat and a kerchief. Gabe thought his "look" was impressive, and he hoped for high-topped boots so he could tuck the pants legs in.

Just as Gabe was modeling his Nat Stein costume, Mr. Nelson's five minute warning bell sounded. Gabe needed to change back into his own clothes, and two of his classmates needed to get the broom and dustpan for hall clean-up duty. However, all three of them were thwarted in their actions, because Gabe had left the door lock on when he pulled the door shut. Mr. Nelson had no key; the custodians probably had a key, but they did not usually lock the door, so it would require a search to find the right key; and Principal Wagner had end-of-the-school-day duties out by the buses. Besides, Mr. Wagner had no key to a janitor closet that was never locked.

Gabe said, "Mr. Nelson, I can't be late; I am supposed to go to a track meet with Coach Crowley. The bus leaves right after the last bell rings!"

Gabe definitely had on "the wrong clothes," but he did have his bag with his track clothes. Between missing the meet in order to hunt the key to unlock the closet or making it to the bus and hence to the track competition even though he had to travel in non-standard attire, Gabe and Mr. Nelson chose the latter.

Mr. Nelson said, "Gabe, wear the costume! You can change into your track clothes in the dressing room at the meet, and if anyone asks you about your unusual garb, you can invite them to come to the Westward Expansion Open House!" Mr. Nelson silently congratulated himself on converting a potential disaster (He knew Coach Crowley would not have been happy if Gabe missed the track meet) into a good advertising opportunity.

"Can I wear the hat, too?" asked Gabe who was always glad for an excuse and permission to wear a hat. Mr. Nelson agreed. Overall, Gabe looked like a stagecoach driver except for the fact that they had not yet located boots that would work so Gabe made his dash to the bus carrying his gym bag, wearing his whole costume, and missing footgear except for socks! Mr. Nelson made a mental note to advertise future history open house events by means of a costumed character parading around the school.

The episode of the locked janitor's closet was a memorable ten minutes at the end of a school day, but it was one that served to build self-esteem for Gabe. He was connected to the Westward Expansion Open House project; in fact, he became a representative of the whole endeavor for Mr. Nelson. He drew attention as someone unique and special as he hurried to the bus wearing his flat brimmed hat and letting the yellow duster swirl around his legs as he walked. He had the power to explain to Mr. Wagner that he was supposed to be wearing the hat based on Mr. Nelson's request, and though he could not articulate it himself, he had just experienced the example of a teacher who modeled how to find a positive solution to circumstances that could have turned into a disaster.

֍

As preparations for the Open House continued, Gabe showed Mr. Nelson a poem he had discovered that was written by the real Overland Stagecoach driver Nat Stein. The poem had been published in the *Montana Post*, April 8, 1865:

I sing to everybody, in the country and the town,
A song upon a subject that's worthy of renown;
I haven't got a story of fairyland to broach,
But plead for the cause of sticking to the box seat of a coach.

Statesmen and warriors, traders and the rest,
May boast of their professions, and think it is the best;
Their state I'll never envy, I'll have you understand,
Long as I can be a driver on the jolly "Overland."

The poem, which continued through several more verses, gave Mr. Nelson one more idea for how to showcase students. He called the home of Jess Woods. Jess was a sophomore at the high school, but he was a former student of Mr. Nelson's, and Mr. Nelson knew that Jess could play a guitar and just about any other stringed instrument. That knowledge had proved to be a hook for interesting Jess in his school work when Mr. Nelson needed him to do class assignments. He had showcased Jess's talents back when Jess was one of his middle school students, and that had helped build a relationship between the two of them so that Jess would do what Mr. Nelson asked of him even if that included studying, researching, or writing reports. For the open house, Mr. Nelson shared the Overland Stagecoach poem and asked Jess to write his own original music to go with the hundred and fifty year old lyrics. Jesse did exactly that and then came on the day of the event and performed the piece for the open house audience. Gabe got to introduce Jess and the song; in the costume and person of Nat Stein he said, "This is the poem I wrote about being an Overland Stagecoach driver."

The Westward Expansion Open House with the traveling museum exhibit, research displays, and student performances had been set up in the middle school's all purpose room, and Mr. Nelson was glad to be able to honor Jess's talent, showcase the work of all of his students, and build relationships with parents who got to see and hear what things their students had been learning.

As the evening concluded and students cleared away their exhibits, and the custodian was helping to put away tables, Mr. Nelson was stopped in his progress when he came upon a big sticky spill of soda in the hallway just outside the exhibit area. "Oh, no!" he exclaimed. "Look at this, who…?"

But his question was cut short by words from Emma, one of the seventh grade girls, "Don't worry Mr. Nelson, Anthony has gone to get a mop. He didn't spill the pop, but he is going to clean it up."

"Good for him!" said Mr. Nelson, and he really meant it. Anthony's taking the initiative to care for the school premises when it was not even a mess of his own making was an example of good citizenship that was just about at the top of Mr. Nelson's personal objectives for what he wanted his students "to know and be able to do" at the end of the school year.

※

For Rachel Mullins, her first year of teaching had been stressful and challenging as she learned the balancing act of covering all the many areas of teaching that were her responsibility, but she had been as thrilled as the students when they began to understand reading in the months right after Christmas. It had been a pleasure to see them blossom and become excited about being able to read.

One day, near the end of the last class period, one of the first graders, little Ashley, who was the P.E. coach's daughter, came back in Rachel's classroom to wait on her dad. When Rachel glanced up, Ashley was doing her Mrs. Mullin's impression because she was in Rachel's chair near the rug where the class always sat for their morning routine, and Ashley was reading a book on patience. It was a book Rachel had read to the class before, but she was certain that Ashley was actually reading the book now rather than just reciting the words from memory. The book told of planting a seed then watering it and waiting for the seed to finally sprout and grow. When Ashley finished the book and flipped it shut, she said, "And that's what patience is!"

Rachel was jolted with a fresh understanding of how important her actions and even her tone of voice were, because, clearly, Ashley and her classmates were using Rachel as a model. It was a point she herself had made to the high school students who had been coming to Lavonia Berber Elementary to work with the first graders on memorizing their speaking parts for the spring program. She knew her students would copy not just the words of play lines, but also the attitudes, expressions, and delivery of the older students. It had been a truly beneficial arrangement because the upper classmen were providing a useful service; it was a way they could make a difference; and the first graders benefitted from the extra coaching from the "Big Kids" whom they considered celebrities.

The weather was tending towards soft spring days that were enticing students to think of outdoor recess. Rachel recognized their urge to break free from the classroom. She even realized that some of her students came to school tired because they or their older brothers and sisters had been participating in spring soccer, softball, baseball, or livestock shows so that they had missed their usual bedtime. Rachel needed to enhance what she knew of classroom management, so she consulted her colleagues for advice on interactive, hands-on class enterprises to keep every child looking, thinking, and learning.

Because of the high mobility of some families, there were children added to the class roles even late in the school year. That's when the elementary creed was helpful to Rachel:

> I am a Lavonia Berber student.
> I believe I am a smart and capable student.
> I will be responsible for my own actions.
> I will treat others nicely.
> I will strive to do better today than I did yesterday.

Rachel showed the creed to the new students and said, "This is how we act."

It helped all the children to learn more smoothly because there was less need to deal with problems. She also took the extra step of providing handouts for any child who was unable to keep up with the pace of the lesson. New students who were unfamiliar with the routine and the material were able to follow lessons by circling words, highlighting terms, or filling in blanks.

Rachel also joined the other elementary teachers in fulfilling a request from Principal Aransus. They set about writing positive referral notes to the principal to describe some good behavior or accomplishment of their students. Mrs. Aransus made a plan to respond to the students who had been given a positive referral, and Rachel took time to write to parents. Reinforcing positive behaviors rather than reprimanding negative ones was elevating the mood for everyone for the final weeks of school.

As the first graders began studying the American Revolution, Rachel wanted to discuss with the class the role of King George of England. In order to discuss kings, she posted a K – W – L Chart for which the students were to list what they already Knew, what they Wanted to know, and what they had already Learned. As the students considered things to list in the categories, several of the things they "knew" about kings were drawn from Simba, the Disney *Lion King*. But then, Rachel asked the class to speak about what new things they wanted to know about kings. The class was quiet until a petite, dark-headed little girl raised her hand.

"Yes, Arianna?" said Rachel.

"Mrs. Mullins and class," began Arianna with importance, "what I want to know is whether a king has a person to put the pillow under his feet for him or if he has to do that himself."

"Thank you, Arianna; you are thinking! We'll write that on the chart," said Rachel. She was smiling to herself. The children were indeed thinking and, in fact, thinking quite originally. She would never have come up with the query about a "pillow servant," and she also admired the proper class procedure of Arianna's competence in addressing her by name and speaking in complete sentences. She and the students had come a long way since last August, and she was finding her role as a teacher more rewarding than ever.

"Far and away the best prize that life has to offer is the chance to work hard at work worth doing."
THEODORE ROOSEVELT

Chapter 9

Learning Up to the Last Minute

"The barriers are not erected which can say to aspiring talents and industry, 'Thus far and no farther.'"
LUDWIG VAN BEETHOVEN

Significant rain storms, sunny days which transformed trees and lawns to lush greenery, important tests and homework assignments, and the excitement of the last weeks of the school year: that was the month of May. At Center City Middle School, Principal Wagner had directed teachers to conduct their own call to excellence through sessions in their classrooms rather than having all-school assemblies during the final month of the school term. The teachers chose different names for the bit of time used to unite the focus of the students for the day, but since it happened in five minutes or less, some teachers called it their "First Five." The agenda for the morning focus time in Gabe's seventh grade class with Mrs. Wilson included a lineup of short activities: flag salute, quote of the day, news and reminders, and celebrations of wacky holidays such as "Tuba Day" and "No Socks Day." Different students had the opportunity to lead the short little business meeting to kick off the work of the school day. On the day it was his turn to be a leader, Gabe gave the new vocabulary word of *collywobbles* and told that it meant "a feeling of fear, apprehension, or nervousness," although his classmates were certain that Gabe himself never experienced collywobbles. Lowell announced which classmates had earned kudos for their track meet successes. Brianna chose to talk about the life principle of service; it was their thirty-third life principle of the year. She used the Douglas M. Lawson quotation: "Serving the needs of others is the light that brightens each day."

As part of the morning's routine, Mrs. Wilson took the lunch count. She would reveal the menu and ask which students planned to eat cafeteria food that day. She had long ago abandoned the practice of merely reading the menu and had resorted to using her flair for drama to give the menu in the voice of some character: perhaps she would be Scarlett O'Hara, a hillbilly, a Russian spy, a Western cowboy, or some other personage who came to mind. One of Gabe's classmates, Danny Gray, had slipped along quietly all year long – in the background. He was never a troublemaker, but he always let the more vivacious and loquacious students take the forefront in whatever activity was going on. "Gray" seemed to be his personality description as well as his name. But on one morning after a particularly engaging First Five, Mrs. Wilson gave the lunch menu, in the style of an operatic recitative.

"Would you like a baked potato?" she sang dramatically.

To her surprise, Danny Gray burst out singing a solo in a matching recitative style, "Yes, I would!"

Mrs. Wilson gave him one of her happiest smiles; she was delighted, not by Danny's acceptance of a baked potato, but by this action which demonstrated his newly developed confidence and comfort in the classroom environment.

"He will be ready to take on the challenges of eighth grade next year!" she thought. Danny's growth in self-assurance wasn't accidental. It had come about through the school culture that was consciously planned to nurture students' self-esteem.

༄༅

Gabe, though he wasn't suddenly singing his lunch menu choice, had a healthy personal self-confidence himself, and his mind was already on his zoo project. Several of his teachers had collaborated on a seventh grade project which was planned to be related to the real world and to integrate math, science, geography, composition, and art. The seventh graders were designing their own zoo, and the teachers had given clear instructions to help them all succeed. Each student chose an animal, researched its natural habitat, food requirements, and behaviors. Then they were to layout enclosures, done to scale, of adequate space with shelter for housing their zoo specimens in a manner which was safe for the animals and for zoo visitors.

Students employed practical applications of math as they calculated the area of each animal's yard and shelter, tallied the expenditures for its food, and added up the costs of any special requirements. Each zoo designer also needed to choose habitat plantings that would replicate the ecology of the animal's home but also assure the flora would thrive in the local climate.

Gabe's mom, Julie, and her sister, Aunt Becca, who was visiting from out of town, were taking advantage of the soft spring weather to go for a Saturday morning walk through the park; they were especially admiring the abundance of blooming irises. Gabe and Jackson were along, but rather than strolling with the ladies, they had created an impromptu soccer game of kicking spiky seed balls which had fallen from the sweet gum trees along the sidewalk. Gabe had already chosen the black rhinoceros as his zoo animal. The choice came easily after the class featured "Rhino Day" as part of First Five on the first of May. He overheard his mom telling Aunt Becca about his project.

"I was able to buy Gabe a model rhinoceros from the Internet for his zoo project," said Julie.

"So, Gabe, is it the right kind of rhinoceros for your project?" called Becca as Gabe made a side dash off the sidewalk to kick the spiky sweet gum ball back into play.

"Yep," said Gabe. "It is a black rhino just like I wanted. Did you know that they are endangered?"

Jackson scuffed the spiky seed ball another eight feet along the sidewalk. "Your rhino model is not black!" he observed.

"That's 'cause black rhinos are really gray. They sometimes look black because they wallow in mud. When the mud dries it protects them from sunburns and insect bites."

"Insect bites?" said Jackson incredulously.

"Yes, you wouldn't think so, but they actually have sensitive skin," said Gabe with the exaggerated inflection of a model on a television commercial touting body lotion.

When they got back home, Aunt Becca got a preview of Gabe's model of the rhino enclosure. He was still working on the map of Africa showing the countries where the black rhino is a native. Mr. Lorrie would give him geography class credit for showing: Kenya, Tanzania, Cameroon, South Africa, Namibia, Zimbabwe, and Angola on the placard which would be part of his project display.

"What foliage are you going to put in your enclosure?" asked Aunt Becca.

Gabe huffed out a sigh. "That's a problem," he said. "Whatever plants I use will probably have to be outside the fence. The rhino would just eat whatever was planted inside! And I have to watch my budget; I don't know how much I can spend on trees and shrubs."

"You have a budget?" said Becca with a note of surprise in her voice.

"Yeah, and rhinos are expensive to buy in the first place, and they are so big that everything to take care of them costs a lot too. But," he exclaimed, "I've got a plan!"

"What's that?" asked Becca.

"There is a kind of bird called an oxpecker. It's also called a tickbird; it hangs out on a rhino and eats ticks and flies and maggots that it finds on the rhino. Isn't that cool? Anyway, I got Lowell to do his project on a tickbird, and he can put his bird in with my rhino, so he won't have any expenses and that means I can use his budget!" said Gabe with a self-satisfied grin.

Aunt Becca laughed. "Quite a clever plan," she said, but she was actually quite impressed with all of the aspects of the zoo project that Gabe seemed to have mastered.

꼬꼬

Besides the zoo project, Mrs. Wilson had asked her students to have memorized three poems. As the school days dwindled down to the last few, she set a deadline for the students to come to her and recite their three poems. It was absolutely a favorite assignment as far as Mrs. Wilson was concerned. The students had come to understand the poems they chose for their focus. She knew many of them would remember their poems long into the future, because when she encountered former students, they often told how much they could still recite. Also, she enjoyed the one-on-one time with the students and being able to look in their eyes and then celebrate with them when they successfully completed their recitations.

Gabe chose Walter D. Wintle's poem "Thinking" for one of his memory pieces. He remembered an activity from the start of school when Mrs. Wilson made "can't" a forbidden word.

"You may say, 'I'm having difficulty with this task' or 'I have never been successful with this kind of a problem before,' but if you say 'I can't' then you are likely to believe that you can't!" she had explained.

So on his day for recitation, he stood before Mrs. Wilson, looked her in the eye and said:

> If you think you're beaten, you are.
> If you think you dare not, you don't.
> If you'd like to win,
> But you think you can't,
> It's almost a cinch you won't.
>
> If you think you'll lose, you're lost,
> For out in the world you'll find
> Success begins with a fellow's will,
> It's all in the state of mind.
>
> If you think you're outclassed, you are.
> You've got to think high to rise.
> You've got to be sure of yourself before
> You can ever win a prize.
>
> Life's battles don't always go
> To the stronger or faster man,
> But soon or late, the man who wins,
> Is the one who thinks he can.

Mrs. Wilson was as pleased as Gabe with his success, and they joined one another in celebrating. She appreciated the demonstration of his memorization, his poise in delivering the piece, and most especially the fact that he remembered and respected her advice about avoiding the self-fulfilling prophecy of saying "I can't."

Principal Aransus was following up on a new plan she had devised for displaying the GE Life Principles for the Lavonia Berber students. She had the student who was the high school yearbook photographer visit the elementary school and take candid pictures of students throughout a school day. Then she looked through the array of photos and found shots of Lavonia Berber students that fit each of the life principles. Her plan was to have the pictures converted into posters for the hallways for the next school year. As teachers and students discussed the definitions and applications of those important character traits, each one would be illustrated by a member of the Lavonia Berber student body. Their poster pictures would remain in the hallways for all of next year to be reminders to everyone to practice the life principles every day.

Jackson and his classmate Ella were photographed in an action shot from gym class. Jackson's face was intent as he concentrated on grabbing the relay race baton from Ella before he made a dash to the north end of the gym. The students didn't actually call it the north end of the gym because the PE Coach had just recently launched a new strategy for integrating geography into PE class. The center court line had been renamed the Equator, and the lines that were meant to mark the difference between the defense zone and the attack zone for volleyball games that the sixth graders played had become the Tropic of Cancer and the Tropic of Capricorn. The far north and south ends of the gym where the volleyball players stood to serve the ball were now called the Polar Regions. So for the day's races of carrying the relay batons from one end of the gym to the other, one teammate started in a Polar Region, dashed across a Temperate Zone, met his relay partner in the Torrid Zone, and handed off the relay baton. That partner continued through the Temperate Zone in the other hemisphere in order to reach the opposite Polar Region. It was a fast-paced and energetic game, and soon all the elementary gym class students had the names for the regions on the globe and their relative locations well in mind.

Mrs. Aransus was particularly well pleased with the stop-action picture showing Jackson's and Ella's intent expressions as they concentrated on handing off the relay baton as they ran at their full speed. She considered it the ideal image to go on the new poster for the life principle of cooperation. Jackson and Ella were cooperating for sure, and cooperation and all the other life principles were part of Coach Hunter's elementary PE classes. Besides his diligence in integrating subject matter into his PE classes, he also promoted the Great Expectations Eight Expectations, and if there were ever any lapse in student behavior, Coach was quick to give reminders of the applicable expectation: "We will not laugh at or make fun of a person's mistakes nor use sarcasm or putdowns." "We will use good manners, saying 'please,' 'thank you,' and 'excuse me' and allow others to go first." "We will help one another whenever possible." "We will recognize every effort and applaud it." "We will encourage each other to do our best." The PE classes were especially good at applying the expectation which said, "We will cheer each other to success." There was always considerable cheering!

After P.E. class, Jackson hurried to change out of his gym shoes and into his clothes for going home. He was in a rush because this was the day he had permission to go with Mrs. Stevens to release some of the animals that had been living in her room during the school year. It was time for those creatures to return to the wild. Mrs. Stevens drove to a nearby state park where there was the right habitat to welcome the two lizards and a tarantula which had been in Mrs. Stevens's classroom all year.

Jackson visited with Mrs. Stevens for the entirety of the trip. He told her about Callie and Big Gray, which was information he had already shared with her, but she celebrated with him anyway when he got to the part of the report that told of the Valentine picture he had received showing the two cats enjoying their new opportunity to be housecats – inside in a warm house when the weather was cold and snowy. He also shared what he had learned about the black rhino from Gabe's zoo project. "Did you know that a rhino's horn is made like a horse's hoof?" he said, quoting what he had heard in Gabe's report. Then he moved on to conjecture about whether the lizards and the tarantula would prosper without the meals that had been provided for them in the classroom.

Mrs. Stevens didn't have to add much to the conversation, because Jackson had so much to say. When she dropped him off for his ride home with his dad, he said, "Thanks, Mrs. Stevens. I really liked helping you with the animals in your classroom. It was fun."

&

The first grade students in Rachel Mullins's class were still engaged in the lessons that she offered each day. They had been learning to read and were truly excited because of the opportunity to explore the world that had just opened to them as readers. They did not have the "through with school" attitude that some older students adopt as the year winds down.

For the annual music program that parents and school supporters from the community attend, Rachel helped her students learn the simple song "I Want to Be Happy." The lyrics declare "I want to be happy, but I won't be happy till I make you happy, too!" It pleased Rachel to teach the students that song because the sentiment of the words matched what she had been telling her students about "helping one another to success." She was certain her cute first graders stole the show as they belted out their song enthusiastically.

The time was fast approaching when it would be "the last day of school," and she would be hugging her first graders for the last time because when she saw them next, they would be big second graders. It surprised her how much affection she had stored up for her class of students. Teaching had turned out to be a good career choice for her, especially since she had the good fortune to be on the faculty of a Great Expectations elementary school. She was already looking forward to the week in July when she would attend her first Great Expectations Summer Institute. From all that she had already learned, she knew it would super-charge her teaching.

※

The first weekend in May, Julie agreed to travel with Lyle back to his hometown for his high school class reunion. A little more than half of his classmates were in attendance for the catered evening meal at the community center near the high school. Lyle enjoyed reconnecting with old friends, meeting their spouses, and learning what career paths they had pursued. The classmates were almost all recognizable; although Bonnie was a slimmer version of her high school self, and Brad's hair was much sparser than it used to be. Kevin was as good-natured and funny as ever, and Louise's clothing, accessories, and diamond ring evidenced the lucrative careers that she and her husband had pursued.

There soon was a recounting of many "remember when" stories: the bus stuck in a snow drift on the way to the basketball state tournament, the graduation program when a thunderstorm moved in and tipped the decorations over onto the superintendent as he made his speech, and the science teacher's podium hidden by miscreant students above the ceiling tiles in the lab room. The stories of student hi-jinks included numerous accounts involving Carl Wayne Fisher. Carl Wayne had been one of the most popular and good-looking classmates, and even Lyle had a couple of funny stories to share about Carl. But Carl was not at the reunion, and Cynthia, who kept track of everyone's careers and addresses and marital status, reported that

Carl Wayne had died the previous year. He had liver disease, digestive problems, and heart problems all of which were related to the fact that he had been an alcoholic.

Lyle realized, now that he thought about it, that Carl Wayne's antics in high school had been accompanied by disregard for the guidelines of parents, disrespect for teachers, and risky behaviors, including reckless driving and underage drinking. Suddenly, the accounts of Carl Wayne's brash behavior were no longer funny, and Lyle was more pleased than ever that the Center City schools had high standards that were being impressed upon the students. The Great Expectations Life Principles permeated the community, and he saw the benefits among his team at work. They showed integrity and attention to detail that made them valuable workers.

On the drive home, Lyle told Julie, "I'm glad our kids have a chance to grow up with high standards of personal conduct; they won't have a tragic story like Carl Wayne's."

꼿

Sarah was enjoying the conclusion of her senior year of high school. Her friend Melissa had drawn her into the big year-long student council project which was winding to a conclusion as the school year ended. The project was called "C.O.L.E.S.L.A.H." The name was pronounced the same as the name of cabbage salad called coleslaw, but this project, labeled most cleverly by a junior boy, stood for the longer name of Co-operating On Lively Education by Students Lending A Hand. The student council paired upper classmen with lower classmen, and for the first semester, each upper classman had the assignment of getting acquainted with his younger high school partner, celebrating successes with him, and offering words of encouragement. Sarah had helped Melissa pass along the dates of birthdays to C.O.L.E.S.L.A.H. partners.

Now that it was in the final semester of the school year, the roles were reversed, and the lower classmen were looking after the upper classmen by sending encouragement for final tests and cheering on their efforts with college applications and scholarship appeals. For one of the days during the last week that the seniors would be at school, the C.O.L.E.S.L.A.H. partners met to eat lunch together in the cafeteria. Sarah's role as a worker had been to help Melissa decorate the cafeteria tables with small pots of spring flowers which were all blooming cheerfully. At the end of the school day, Sarah, Melissa, and several other student council members took the flowers which had been table decorations and delivered them to teachers with notes of appreciation. That was most timely since it was National Teacher Appreciation Week. Sarah enjoyed the delight that registered on teachers' faces when she walked in to deliver a little flower ready to be planted in a home garden.

Very soon the flurry of activity that accompanies graduation was in full swing. There was a special day of celebration for the seniors, awards programs, preparation for graduation, and then – the final night of graduation.

Lyle and Julie, who were seated with the other parents, were pleased to see the orderly conduct of the commencement program. Then came the announcement that Sarah Hanson was the recipient of the most sizeable scholarship presented that evening.

"Congratulations, honey!" said Julie as she hugged Sarah when she came at the conclusion of the program to give her mom a long-stemmed red rose.

Lyle was beaming; he exclaimed, "Way to go!"

He was proud of Sarah's accomplishment and more than a little pleased that the cost of Sarah's college education would be significantly defrayed by the scholarship.

The Hanson grandparents had come for graduation festivities, and Sarah had a rose for her grandmother, too.

"I'll be right back," said Sarah. "I want to catch Mrs. Trotter and give her a rose."

Soon Sarah spotted her English teacher across the crowded auditorium and made her way through the happy confusion of elated graduates all dressed in their caps and gowns, family and friends offering congratulations to their special seniors, and a few younger siblings like Gabe and Jackson who were mainly glad the program was over.

"Mrs. Trotter," called Sarah when she was near enough for Mrs. Trotter to hear her.

"Oh, Sarah," said Mrs. Trotter, "Congratulations! I am so proud of you. What an accomplishment to be awarded such a special scholarship! You have worked hard this year."

Sarah handed her a rose and said, "I want to thank you. I wouldn't have gotten the scholarship without your help. When I went to the interview, I used our procedure for speaking in complete sentences just like you have had us do in class, and then as I answered the questions that I was asked, I remembered the life principle words that are posted around the walls in your classroom. I used as many of those life principle words as I could. I'm sure that's what made the difference and won me the scholarship. So, thank you!"

Sarah's words of appreciation were concluded with a hug. Her eyes were sparkling with tears because of the occasion which felt so momentous and the sadness to be departing from Center City High School with her classmates and teachers; even so, she felt ready to step up to the next round of challenges. She could hardly recall the reticent, uncertain student she had been last August. Next year would be even better!

"The best endings are the ones that lead to new beginnings."
MATHANGI SUBRAMANIAN

Epilogue

Summary of Successes

"Success is a journey of transformations."
VISHWAS CHAVAN

As the school year arrived at the festivities of graduation in May, the Hanson family children all found themselves far advanced in their educational journey from their starting points in August.

Jackson, who had been distraught with the move to Center City because he had to leave his cats behind, discovered teachers who nurtured his special competencies and provided opportunities based on his affinity for animals. Mrs. Johnson had recognized his interests and honored him by called him a zoologist; Mrs. Stevens, who wasn't even his classroom teacher, gave him the responsibility to care for her classroom rabbits. Just as the last day of school approached, he made the acquaintance of a lively gray tabby kitten that lived next door. He was proud of the accomplishments of his learning through the year, and it was going to be a good summer.

At Sarah's high school graduation program, the parents of Jackson's classmate Ella Duncan had worked their way to where the Hansons were seated and introduced themselves.

With a warm smile, Mrs. Duncan said, "We have been hoping to meet you."

"Oh?" replied Julie.

"Yes, we wanted especially to meet Jackson. Ever since he gave Ella eighteen cards in her Valentine box, we have heard many reports from her about all that Jackson does!"

Julie glanced over at Jackson who had been listening to the conversation. He grinned and couldn't keep his dimples from showing. He really didn't mind being "famous" in the Duncan household.

※

Gabe had started the year with a sense of loss because there was to be no soccer at the new school. He thrived on throwing his energy into physically being on the move and had been certain that he was doomed to the requirement to sit still much longer than he could tolerate. But, at Center City Middle School, he had been given many opportunities to learn through being up and doing and moving. His teachers' provision of kinesthetic learning opportunities had helped him learn and be successful. Besides that, since the family had moved to a new community, he had begun school in August without knowing a single other student, much less having anyone to count as a friend. By May, if he were asked, he would say that the best part of the year had been the many new friends he had gained. A bonus of those new relationships was the fact that they were all friends who joined him in following the character-building life principles instilled by his teachers and the school's climate of mutual respect. He enjoyed the sense of competence that he had gained, and though summer vacation was going to be great, he would be ready for the high expectations that he would meet as an eighth grader.

※

Sarah could hardly realize how far she had progressed in the school year. Like Gabe, she enjoyed the new friendships she had formed, and counted on many of those amicable attachments to stretch into her days as a college freshman. She was especially glad that Sam Goodwin had made sure he had her email address.

Yet, the most striking impact on her life as a student was the scholastic growth she had experienced. It gave her a sense of power as she launched into higher education. She had learned so much. In fact, she had learned more than she ever intended, more than she realized, more than she previously thought she would ever need to know!

※

For Julie, the sorrow she had felt in August that her children were missing out on being a part of an educational system with school pride and a sense of community had all dissipated as she watched the functioning of the school. Activities involved the whole student population in contributing to the good of the school and making a difference for one another. Accomplishments were recognized and celebrated; students had a voice in the conduct of events. The school citizens cheered for the teams in all the sports competitions, and Julie was particularly appreciative of the respectful treatment of the flag when it was presented formally by the honor guard. Her children were gaining the heritage of a school with high academic expectations and a culture that was a model of good citizenship. It was all she could have wished.

※

Lyle was truly pleased, not just with the school pride or "school spirit," but with the high standards of character he saw developing in his children. He was glad that Sarah had learned the lesson of upholding her responsibilities to the drama cast when she came close to ditching dress rehearsal in order to go on a date. And, he expected that Jackson and Gabe would grow into young men who had integrity along with the creativity and gumption to find a solution when faced with complications. They were becoming the kind of men he wanted to have as employees.

In June, after school was out, Rachel Mullins attended Great Expectations Summer Institute with several other teachers from Lavonia Berber Elementary School. Mrs. Aransus went along as well, attending the class for principals. Rachel was already well aware of Great Expectations practices because of the instruction she had received from colleagues and the GE Coach, but the Summer Institute class was thoroughly enjoyable and beneficial. By the third day of the four-day session, she was feeling overwhelmed, but it was a good kind of overwhelmed because she was gathering so many ideas, and they were all plans and strategies which she wanted to implement in her own classroom.

She enjoyed the new friends who were participants in the class with her. One older teacher, who could boast many years of teaching experience, was still finding useful help from the training. "Great Expectations validates my own values and is giving me a way to organize the things I want to share with my students," she said.

Lance, who was also a member of Rachel's class sessions, wore boots and jeans and pearl-button shirts and charmed everyone with his folksy cowboy lingo. He admitted freely that he had not wanted to attend GE Summer Institute.

"I did not want to give up my summer days to come sit in some class. But then I got here, and everyone was smiling, and now I'm just as happy as they are to be here. I guess I am smiling, too!"

∽∼

The numerous accounts of Great Expectations teachers, administrators, and students which formed the basis for this book are only a part of *The Great Expectations Story*. There is too much to tell. In order to get the rest of the story, you will need to visit a Great Expectations School, attend GE Summer Institute, and, perhaps, even become a Great Expectations practitioner yourself!

∽∼

Charlie Hollar, the founder of Great Expectations, often visited schools, and on one occasion when he interviewed students where GE had been newly implemented, he got just the response he wanted to hear from one student.

"What does Great Expectations mean to you?" Charlie asked the students.

One seventh grade girl replied, "I learned more this year than I ever had before, and I think, also, Great Expectations made me a better person!"

That's the essence of *The Great Expectations Story*.

"GE transforms lives through education."

The Great Expectations Tree

As Great Expectations became an entity, Charlie Hollar, the Foundation Board, and the GE Leadership Team wrestled with identifying an appropriate logo and slogan to represent the mission of the group. They recognized the amazing changes in young people as they grow from their first days of school as small children to confident and competent graduates, so the saying, "From little acorns come mighty oaks," seemed to fit.

Great Expectations looked to a piece written for the school declamation of a seven year old boy in 1791:

> You'd scarce expect one of my age
> To speak in public on the stage;
> And if I chance to fall below
> Demosthenes or Cicero,
> Don't view me with a critic's eye,
> But pass my imperfections by.
> Large streams from little fountains flow,
> *Tall oaks from little acorns grow.*
> These thoughts inspire my youthful mind
> To be the greatest of mankind;
> Great, not like Caesar, stained with blood,
> But only great as I am good.

Great Expectations adopted the image of a mighty oak tree and added the slogan "Tall oaks from little acorns grow…" Today the tree is still the mark of Great Expectations. The phrase that encapsulates the focus of GE has been enhanced to the expression "Transforming Lives Through Education."

Want to Know More?

Great Expectations offers…
- Training that affirms educators and **inspires** them to seek ever higher plateaus of **accomplishment** with their students.
- Training that enables educators to help their students achieve **success** on required standards in a **safe** and **enjoyable** learning environment.
- Training that guides educators in developing **noble** young citizens who are **thoroughly equipped** for the life challenges in our rapidly changing world.

This research-based training is provided through
Great Expectations Summer Institute
and through many professional development opportunities offered throughout the year including instructional support from Great Expectations Coaches at school sites and Leadership Academy for school and district administrators.

To learn more, go to www.greatexpectations.org
Or call (918) 444 3744

Follow the links on the website to
- See **Great Expectations Education Foundation** on Facebook for daily instruction tips from professional journals.
- Follow GE on Twitter.
- Watch GE videos on YouTube.
- See pictures of GE events on Google+

൭൰൫

Great Expectations guides educators in developing
Academic Excellence in a *Culture of Respect*

About the Author

Christy Sheffield is an educator who taught high school English, speech, drama, and German during her twenty-five years in the classroom. She utilized Great Expectations Practices in her own classroom and later became part of the GE Leadership Team. She has been a presenter at national conferences in California, Florida, Illinois, and Texas.

As a drama coach, she directed over 60 plays, many of which she wrote to suit the talents and interests of her students. She translated that experience into the writing of *The Great Expectations Story* because she has woven together the examples of Great Expectations in operation by telling them as the experiences of a fictional family.

She has been honored as a finalist for State Teacher of the Year, as an Oklahoma Foundation for Excellence Secondary Teacher of the Year, and as a Christa McAuliffe Fellow. She was among the very first National Board Certified Teachers in the nation. As a pioneer implementer of educational technology, she conducted humanities classes over interactive educational television.

Christy is involved in an ongoing project to write children's books to teach the Great Expectations Life Principles. So far, the books include *Wondering* (courage), *Perseverance Pays Off* (perseverance), *Braving Difficulties* (courage), *Bill and Coo* (friendship), *Consider the Consequences* (common sense), *Use Your Patience* (patience), and *Good Citizen Jack* (citizenship).